The Library Administration Series

Lowell A. Martin, General Editor

Scarecrow

Library

Administration

Series

No. 3

Participatory Management in Libraries

DONALD J. SAGER

The Scarecrow Press, Inc.
Metuchen, N.J., & London
1982

Library of Congress Cataloging in Publication Data

Sager, Donald J., 1938–
  Participatory management in libraries.

  (Scarecrow library administration series; no. 3)
  Bibliography: p.
  Includes index.
  1. Library administration—United States.
2. Employees' representation in management—
United States.   I. Title.   II. Series.
Z678.S23   025.1'0973   82-783
ISBN 0-8108-1530-3   AACR2

CONTENTS

iii

PREFACE

THE SCARECROW PRESS *series on library administration covers both standard aspects of management and newer trends in the field. The present volume on participatory management is in the second category.*

Participatory management has become almost a catch phrase or slogan. We are all for democracy in the workplace. Old-fashioned authoritarian administration is out, we are often told, and participatory management is the wave of the future. As a matter of fact, hierarchial organizations remain and will continue, in libraries as elsewhere; levels of responsibility are integral to large-scale enterprise. On the other side, from the workers' standpoint, it is unrealistic to assume that all employees want to participate in management. As this volume indicates, some simply want to do a good day's work and go home at five o'clock without carrying their agency's problems with them.

Donald Sager sees both side of the prospect. He is a realistic advocate. The potential of participatory management for promoting worker motivation and satisfaction on the job is brought out fully in these pages. More than that, the contribution to the library in increased production is identified, which has particular relevance in a time of financial constraints. At the same time the deterrents, both institutional and individual, are faced squarely. We hear the voice of experience as well as the voice of theory.

For all the repetition of the topic in the professional literature, libraries have adopted participatory management to only a limited extent. Presumably the non-administrative professional and the library clerk are to get job satisfaction from the service rendered and the pay accorded, not from any role in

*planning for their agency. The author examines what efforts
have been made in libraries, and then goes beyond to show
what could be accomplished.*

*The book does not stop with history and definition and
analysis. It goes on to implementation of participatory management in libraries. Chapters are devoted to preparing the
agency and the staff for the change in management style, to
committee and other structures for the purpose, and to the roles
of individual participants. Case studies are presented, showing
workplace democracy in action, in some instances successfully,
in others, not.*

*Particularly interesting is the discussion of economic returns
not just to the agency but also to individual staff members,
which the author sees as possible even in the public sector. He
shows how participatory management can be applied to selected
issues and departments within a library without necessarily
extending to every problem that arises. A wary eye is kept open
for pseudo-participation, those devices that some managers use
to involve the staff without actually delegating any part of
decision making.*

*Donald Sager brings extensive background and experience to
the task. Until recently Commissioner in charge of the Chicago
Public Library, he has been the chief executive officer in four
other libraries: Columbus and Franklin County (Ohio),
Mobile (Alabama), Elyria (Ohio), and Kingston (New York).
He has taught library administration at Kent State University
and the University of Alabama. Finally, he is the current President of the Public Library Association and Distinguished
Visiting Scholar at the Online Computer Library Center.*

*Sager sees participatory management not so much as an
administrative fad but as an opportunity to increase motivation
on the job and to help meet mounting financial constraints
on libraries. Rather than a constraint on the manager, democratization of the workplace opens a source of internal strength
in difficult times. If he is right, all library administrators should
release this potential within their own staffs.*

Lowell A. Martin
Series Editor

INTRODUCTION

To MANAGE effectively, supervisors must have an awareness of the strengths and capabilities of the employees involved in the operation under their direction, and a willingness and ability to employ those capabilities. In some instances an outstanding manager credits success to good judgment of staff members in the organization. In other instances, the administrator may indicate it was knowledge of the job on the part of employees, and the capability to assign the right people to the task. Whatever a successful manager says, it is certain that success rests firmly on the marshalling of staff talents to the completion of an essential responsibility

Unfortunately, not every supervisor can do this. That may not be due to a lack of proficiency on the part of the supervisor, or an unwillingness to dedicate time and energy to the solution of a problem. It may or may not be due to the strengths or weaknesses of the staff assigned to the manager, although a great deal will depend upon the manager's knowledge of those capabilities. The most frequent cause of failure on the part of a supervisor is inability to employ the most effective method in working with assigned staff in completing a task or solving an assigned problem. Simply put, the supervisor is simply unable to use the human resources available for the job.

The work environment is constantly changing, and some managers do not keep sensitive to change and its impact upon employees. Until relatively recently, many managers were products of the Great Depression. They often attained their positions based on a certain degree of proficiency in the craft or profession they supervised. That proficiency may have come from special training or practical working experience that gave them insight and appreciation for that craft or profession. In short, they loved the work. They also valued it, because the absence of it spelled loss of status and security.

While these managers are certainly aware that the existence of unemployment insurance, welfare, and two-income families has altered employee attitudes, they are still often mystified and frustrated by those employees who simply refuse to carry out their directives, even in the face of the supervisor's threat of dismissal. The manager may have a solid knowledge of the job and an array of motivational tools. The employee may have the skills to do the job. Yet, the job is often not done, or done poorly.

As a library director, I have had more than 200 supervisors as my responsibility. Most of them were dedicated and knowledgeable of their field. Many had taken advanced courses to prepare themselves for management responsibilities. To keep them current, our institution regularly invested in special courses for supervisory personnel so they were kept aware of new trends and techniques. Inevitably, they were confronted with management problems which could not be solved using the traditional tools and techniques, or they faced circumstances where the traditional methods could not be employed for various reasons, financial or otherwise.

In helping those supervisors to deal with problems, I became increasingly aware that, while the majority of management problems are caused by personnel, they can best be solved by the very personnel involved with the problem. What frustrates both the supervisor and the employee is certainly work-related in most instances, and often their differing perspectives prevent them from arriving at a method of approaching and dealing with the problem.

This is more than just a problem of communication or a difference in generational attitude. It is a matter of role, and prerogatives. The typical supervisor is developed and trained to employ certain tools and techniques to carry out specified responsibilities. The supervisor can recommend pay increases, or disciplinary actions, allow time off, and use standards and policies to ensure consistency in actions. The employees, in turn, may have a union or certain established policies to protect their interests, and they can express their dissatisfaction with the direction and leadership received by giving only grudging support or refusing to perform the work assigned if they feel it is not part of their job.

The process of sharing responsibilities, and jointly arriving at the methods of coping with common problems, is traumatic to both the supervisor and the employee, for it involves breaking with the rigid roles that evolved in our society between employer and employee over the past one thousand years.

It has been theorized that much of the turmoil that has engulfed labor and management relations during recent decades is due to generational differences. When the employees at the General Motors Lordstown plant went out on strike, rebelling against the mind-numbing automated pace of the assembly line, it was noted that many of the employees were college educated, young people who were not satisfied with just a good paycheck and steady work. The older "company men," who provided the supervision, and who still remembered the Great Depression, could not comprehend the frustration of this newer generation.

Many disagree with that conclusion. They argue that dissatisfaction with the workplace is not a symptom of youth. Rather, it is a symptom of a changing society. It is possible to find just as many situations where the disenchanted worker is the older employee, who is rebelling against yet another loss of control and a denuding of responsibility over assigned work, often by a manager who may not be aware of or sensitive to the outcome. Age is not the reason for labor unrest.

What both the supervisor and the employee are facing is the need to develop new roles and to break some of the traditional prerogatives that were held by both for centuries. The supervisor must learn when and how to gain participation in decision making. The employee must learn that he cannot avoid responsibility for the final outcome of the work. There are also broader implications for society and its institutions in this partnership. If the worker is to be given greater responsibility, then the individual deserves greater recognition and rewards. If the supervisor is to be more effective in this setting, then this individual will be required to learn a new catechism and develop new skills.

The purpose of this book is to review some of the common problems that both the supervisor and the employee face, from the perspective of a practicing library director, and demonstrate how participatory management might contribute as an alternative management technique. To lead into that, and provide some essential background, I will also review briefly some of the predecessor techniques which have evolved during this century. These techniques and their underlying philosophies should provide a better understanding of why and how participatory management evolved, and provide some indication of the path it may take in the future. I would be remiss if I failed to properly define participatory management, and illustrate what it is not.

By and large, this is meant to be a practical guide to the use of this technique in libraries, and will focus more often on examples from this profession, and omit the theoretical aspects. The bibliography will provide direction for those who wish to pursue other aspects of this subject.

Participatory management is certainly not the answer to every pressing issue in librarianship. There are many situations where it would be the entirely wrong path to take in dealing with a problem. For those who attempt to fashion a management style based on this technique, I would provide warning that you will find it lacking. This is only a tool which both labor and management can employ in those settings where both must work together in resolving questions affecting them and the effectiveness of their institution.

Chicago, July 1981

PARTICIPATORY MANAGEMENT IN LIBRARIES

1 THE BACKGROUND

THE PERSON who deserves the credit or blame, depending upon your perspective, for establishing the first modern management technique was born in Germantown, Pennsylvania in 1856.[1] Frederick Winslow Taylor intended to become an engineer, but in his youth he suffered a nervous breakdown which prevented him from entering college. Upon his recovery, Taylor elected to become a machinist with the Midvale Iron Works in Philadelphia.

Distressed by what he felt was a lack of productivity, he was brought to the point of developing several tenets that were to form the foundation for his philosophy of management. These were:

- To examine each and every element of a person's work;
- To carefully hire and educate the employee, based on the analysis of the work;
- To establish a cooperative agreement between the employee and the supervisor which would ensure the most effective method of accomplishing the work;
- To carefully break the work down into equally sized, manageable tasks.

Up until this time, the usual procedure was to hire anyone deemed able-bodied and let them decide which job they wanted, and let them do it as they or their supervisor decided was best. The most memorable product to evolve from Taylor's tenets was the time-and-motion study, which was the

3

method he designed to analyze the tasks, and reorganize them into a more efficient working pattern.

Bethlehem Steel Company soon hired Taylor to help in reorganization of its operations. In one classic example, Taylor demonstrated through time-and-motion study and his management tenets that he could increase the productivity of a laborer named Schmidt. Prior to Taylor's arrival, Schmidt had been able to load only 12½ tons of pig iron a day. However, as a result of careful analysis and supervision, Schmidt was able to increase his productivity to 47½ tons of pig iron per day. No one is quite certain of Schmidt's reaction to this change in his work habits, or the tangible rewards he received. Taylor, on the other hand, advanced rapidly at Bethlehem until he was finally fired over a dispute regarding Taylor's advocacy of greater pay for workers in return for increased productivity. Despite that major heresy, Taylor succeeded in following years through his writings and service as a consultant to industry. His texts established the basis for "scientific management," and gave birth to management as a recognized academic discipline. In fact, in 1915, only five management courses were offered by colleges and universities anywhere in the United States. In less than a decade, every college and university of any pretension offered an array of courses on the subject.

At this same time, Henry Ford was developing his manufacturing techniques, and the tenets espoused by Taylor led to the design of the assembly line and the concept of the worker as an interchangeable part. Management historians refer to this era as the period of mechanistic man and woman. Taylor genuinely believed that workers preferred to function as interchangeable parts, since it relieved them of decision making. In fact, the whole purpose of his management technique was to eliminate decisions in the manufacturing process, since they slowed the pace of production and errors resulted from incorrect decisions reached under the strain of production schedules.

While industry was enraptured with the techniques Taylor developed, there was growing concern about employee unrest. Massive labor strikes drove management to the realization that work standards and $5 per day were not enough to keep the assembly lines running smoothly. One of the first indications of this change in philosophy was the creation in many plants of new positions concerned with safety, personnel, training, and health. They were evidence of a new trend called the human relations movement.

The Hawthorne Experiments

Nothing was more indicative of this trend than the experiments undertaken by Elton Mayo, an industrial sociologist, at the Hawthorne Works of the Western Electric Company in Cicero, Illinois in the late 1920's and early 1930's. Mayo was involved in reaching some conclusions from tests on various lighting levels that were conducted at that plant to determine whether better lighting would improve employee productivity. A positive result could sell a great many more light bulbs to production-conscious executives throughout the world.

Westinghouse kept meticulous records of the experiments, and its management could not understand why the test group of employees who agreed to participate in the experiment showed substantial increases in productivity, whether the lighting levels were increased, decreased, or not changed at all. Mayo determined that lighting had no impact on productivity in this experiment. The increased morale and output was solely related to being involved in a meaningful experience. The attention that was given to them made the workers feel they were doing something that was important.

To verify that conclusion, Mayo gained the approval of Westinghouse to try various changes in hours as well as lighting. These tests were conducted upon 20,000 workers, and it confirmed Mayo's earlier conclusions. A greater expression of concern for the employee on the part of management would result in greater productivity. From this study and subsequent writings, management and government introduced many changes in the workplace which are taken for granted today, such as social security, pension plans, vacations, paid holidays, sick pay, and tuition reimbursement.

Employers began to accept the fact that workers were more

often affected by other workers, and that the social environment was as important as decent working conditions. The era of social man and woman in the workplace had arrived, replacing the time-and-motion study, and the mechanistic view of the employee. Another element was soon discovered in the human relations movement, however, that gave management cause for concern. If the social environment was an important factor, and people were affected by their fellow workers, then, to ensure acceptance by their co-workers they might be just as willing to restrict their output as to increase it. The emotional needs of the worker gave rise to yet another specialty in industry, the employee counselor.

Psychological Theories

The next stage in management theory was directly influenced by a pantheon of management consultants and academicians who developed a collective foundation for what has become known variously as job enrichment, quality of work, humanization of work, or job redesign.

Foremost among the leaders of this movement is Frederick Herzberg. He based his theory upon two archetypes, or definitions of man, which he borrowed from the Old Testament—Adam and Abraham.[2] Herzberg visualized Adam as a lazy animal, only slightly differentiated from that state by his capability for perceiving an infinite variety of pain. Adam is further handicapped because he is cursed with the ability to perceive pain in three dimensions—past, present, and future. He can remember pain, feel present pain, and anticipate future pain. He or she prevails in the work environment because of that characteristic. Borrowing from the pioneer psychologist Abraham Maslow and his hierarchy of needs, Herzberg typified Adam as seeking to avoid pain through his concern for security, safety, good working conditions, salary, and fringe benefits. Herzberg coined the phrase "hygiene factors" to describe these elements. They are the powerful motivators which traditionally have been used as the tools of management.

Turning to the other archetype, Abraham, Herzberg called

our attention to the fact that this personality was unique in the Old Testament. Abraham had a covenant, or contract with God. The contract provided for certain responsibilities which belonged to God, and the balance which belonged to Abraham. Here is a figure, indeed, who is not worried about pay or fringe benefits, or any of the hygiene factors that so concerned Adam. Abraham is motivated by other goals, which he has established for himself.

Herzberg concluded that management has to concern itself with the hygiene factors if it is to have a solid foundation on which to motivate its employees, but it must also turn its attention to the job itself, and allow the employee some growth and value in it. Herzberg's theories were tested by a manpower utilization specialist for American Telephone and Telegraph named Robert N. Ford in the mid-1960's in an effort to retain more of the bright recruits that company had gathered from the nation's colleges and universities. [3]

The classic example was provided in a test of 120 women in the complaint department at AT&T. A relatively high turnover in this department, involving college graduates with potential for advancement in management, and a relatively fixed job routine, met the essential ingredients for the test. It was decided that the hygiene factors associated with the jobs would not be altered; all that would be changed was the job itself. A control group was established, and a time long enough to ensure that "Hawthorne effect" elements did not influence the results was determined.

Ford and his staff, working with the supervisors, decided to alter the test group's job through various vertical and horizontal job loading techniques. The vertical loading was accomplished through an increase in the work load. Horizontal job loading was achieved through broadening the work responsibility so the individual performed more than one function. Participation in deciding how the work was to be organized was developed, supervision was decreased, and flexibility was introduced in assignments.

The results revealed a substantial decrease in employee turnover in the test group. Only one employee left, and the reason was her reluctance to assume greater responsibility.

Morale increased in the test group, and more workers qualified for promotion because of the increased experience they gained. Concern turned from hygiene factors to willingness to tackle management problems. As a result of the experience, AT&T subsequently instituted a major program—called the Work Itself Program—which focused on job enrichment as a means of reducing turnover and improving productivity.

Another major figure in management theory is Douglas MacGregor, whose theory X and Y has influenced managers for more than a generation.[4] MacGregor adopted these labels because of his intent to arrive at as neutral a name as possible for two diverse management techniques. He wanted to avoid preference for either. In theory X the manager must visualize the worker as antagonistic, or lazy, somewhat akin to the Adam archetype used by Herzberg. Theory Y demands that the manager consider the worker as an individual with a need for growth, relating to Herzberg's image of Abraham. Theory Y managers are those who invite the participation of their employees in decisions affecting their job. It does not mean complete freedom in the jobplace, but involves the employee in those elements where democracy is possible, and where contributions can be meaningfully applied.

Theory X managers are not necessarily typified by regular use of the lash. The emphasis in their style is upon discipline to achieve harmony and teamwork. MacGregor was quick to point out that many employees only respond to authority and do not wish to participate in decision-making.

The contribution made by MacGregor to management was the identification of management styles and the realization that flexibility was essential, dependent upon the situation and the individual. That concentration upon the individual and the recognition of the differences which exist was a marked contrast to other theories which prescribed a uniform style in directing and motivating personnel.

Chris Argyris represents another contributor to management theory which led to participatory management.[5] Argyris devoted his attention to the built-in obsolescence evident in many organizations. Most of his attention was directed toward industry and the problem created by repetitive tasks, but his work was to have a universal influence upon all types of organizations. Argyris concluded that almost every study made of assembly-line workers reported their frustration and lack of motivation. The traditional method used by industry to motivate these workers, namely salary, did not work after the employees' basic needs were met. The nominal gains in productivity which were achieved through greater pay incentives were only accomplished at very high cost.

To deal with the problem Argyris convinced management to grant more responsibility to each of the workers in the assembly, often to the extent of assigning full responsibility for completion of an entire unit to a single employee. Experience in various settings supported his theory that while production levels dropped temporarily because of the learning curve the employee had to progress through, the original level of production was soon re-established, with definite gains in employee morale and motivation. Lower absenteeism and turnover were also evident as the work responsibility broadened through vertical loading.

Several Swedish industries began implementing job enrichment and participation in the early 70's as one means of coping with motivational and attendance problems.[6] Automakers SAAB and Volvo announced that they were breaking away from traditional assembly-line production. Both were influenced in their decision by annual employee turnover rates of 30 to 40 per cent of their total labor force. In one year, SAAB reported the necessity to replace 100 per cent of its assembly-line force. Both companies were unable to recruit enough Swedish workers for production activities, and they had to draw large numbers of employees from foreign countries.

Subsequent reports of this experience revealed that production costs did increase, and the alternatives developed through the participation of supervisors and workers required more time. Despite this negative aspect, both companies are continuing with the technique. No longer considered an experiment, the methods are being extended to even the traditional assembly-line plants that the companies operate. Among the positive aspects were reduced absenteeism and turnover, better workflow, higher quality end product, smoother labor-management relations, greater employee initiative and sense of responsibility, improved new employee recruiting, and improved community relations.

Job enrichment is not without its critics, who are quick to point out that not every change will necessarily solve labor problems. A person whose normal job involves washing dishes is not particularly enriched by being given responsibility to wash the silverware. Not all work can be enhanced, and while management constantly seeks to automate out of existence those jobs that no one wants, those jobs remain because the labor market permits.

Factors in Job Satisfaction

Fundamental to those theorists who have shaped job reform as a major management trend during the 1970's is a hierarchy of factors influencing job satisfaction among workers. The first of these is achievement. Without this sense of accomplishment, most theorists agree that employees cannot be motivated, or can be motivated only at great cost to the organization. In a library application, it would be possible to identify those positions which offer the greatest sense of accomplishment, and those which offer little. In that context, the clerical, page, and technical processes positions usually present the greatest management challenge, but are often the most ignored. That is where turnover and absenteeism is greatest.

One of the assumptions on which online shared cataloging was based was that it would result in a decrease in the number of clerical and professional positions in technical service departments. Instead, many clerical positions were upgraded. The end result, although not intended, was job enrichment for a job classification normally not considered likely to benefit from automation. While that experience did not extend to an analysis of changes in turnover and absenteeism rates, it would be of value to gather that information to see if the experience is similar to that of industry.

Another element considered essential to motivation by the

theorists is recognition or appreciation by the employee's superiors or co-workers.[7] One of the enriching elements to the employees involved in the Hawthorne experiments, for example, was the impression that their experience would contribute significantly to employee relations. We commonly expect that our contributions to our profession will also achieve some recognition by our colleagues, and contribute to the advancement of our profession. And the person who fails to respond positively to a compliment regarding his work is most rare.

A third element is the work itself. If you are an individual who enjoys books and helping people draw upon those resources to meet their needs, then obviously you will enjoy serving as a librarian. Conversely, if you feel inadequate in that role, surrounded by resources which are unfamiliar to you, and reluctant to serve those who you consider antagonistic or crude, then your satisfaction in that endeavor will be low, and motivation might only be achieved through identification of some aspect of that profession which more closely matches your interests.

A fourth element common to the theories of those concerned with job democratization is a desire for increased responsibilities. Indeed, without this assumption, the whole foundation of the job-enrichment movement crumbles. It is here that critical failures have most often been observed, for while some employees may desire responsibility for some portion of their work, they prefer to abdicate responsibility for all elements. Herzberg has argued that the failure is not in the theory, in these instances, but in the method the manager may have employed. Be that as it may, each manager must be sensitive to those elements of responsibility for the task which the employee wishes to evade.

The enlargement of the job, or horizontal loading, should not be considered as an end in itself, but rather as a means for developing the individual so he or she can grow in the organization. The supervisor who enriches the job by delegating greater and greater responsibility owes the individual an opportunity for advancement and recognition for his or her achievement. This is the fifth element in this hierarchy.

In many respects, pay or additional fringe benefits may be

welcome, and are essential to maintaining morale. But they are not sufficient incentive in participatory management. It is only when the individual is admitted to full partnership, and has official recognition of this fact, that motivation can fully occur.

A final element common to each theory of job reform is the opportunity for growth. Those organizations which experience the greatest problem in this respect, according to Argyris, are those which are stagnant, where new development is not occurring, and where new ideas are supressed. This is why relatively stable organizations experience high turnover, often of the most creative talent. It is not sufficient for an organization to constantly seek out and recruit new qualified personnel. The more difficult aspect is to establish those avenues and strategies that will ensure these individuals being given challenges and authority and resources. A dynamic organization will attract and retain dynamic personnel, if they are given an opportunity to contribute.

In summary, the factors essential for job satisfaction are achievement, recognition, the relationship of the work to the individual's interests, increasing responsibility, advancement and growth. While any organization can survive without those elements, the cost is likely to be high in terms of morale, turnover, absenteeism, retraining and over the long term the result will be an organization which will become obsolete in satisfying the needs of its clientele.

Deterrents to Job Satisfaction

There is a reverse side to this coin, namely an appraisal of those elements of the job which are likely to cause the greatest dissatisfaction, according to many of the job-enrichment theorists. The first of these is a pervasive attitude of restriction. Institutions which fall into this category possess a heavy supervisory presence, where decisions are reviewed at levels much higher than would be appropriate, and where policies and procedures are inherently top-down and top heavy.

In the library setting, a public service librarian whose hands are continually tied by repressive and excessively restrictive lending policies which create public antagonism is not likely to enjoy his or her role. Interpreting these policies to the public when there is little understanding or sympathy for them on the part of the staff is certain to create negative public relations. The library which does not involve those staff members in the decision-making process in the design and maintenance of public service policies is an institution that deserves the criticism it is certain to receive from its clients.

The only type of supervision which is detested more than repression is incompetence. While most theorists in job reform promote democratic supervision, they are uniform in condemning the extreme situation where the supervisor totally abdicates responsibility. Without adequate supervision providing guidance, training, and support no employee can feel confident in assuming greater responsibility in the decision-making process.

Where hesitation exists among employees to participate in management, it is often based on the fear that a mistake will be held fully against them, and where a weak supervisor is attempting to sidestep a difficult decision that he or she should make. Several years ago, a branch head in a public library system was removed by his director because of his misuse of participatory management on disciplinary questions. Whenever an employee arrived late, he would convene a committee of his staff to decide the disciplinary action to be taken against the offender. The staff were not asked to establish the policy, but were only required to administer it by a supervisor reluctant to exercise his responsibilities, and incapable of judging when to waive the policy because of mitigating circumstances.

Poor interpersonal relationships are a third factor in job dissatisfaction. One of the most common grounds for transfer in many organizations is incompatibility, and it is the most vexing for a supervisor. The personnel selected for a unit might have all of the skills and experience required for success, but personality differences may be the basis for mutual or individual dissatisfaction. The dilemma the supervisor faces in these situations is to risk continual conflict in an effort to avoid displacement of an employee who has no job-related deficiencies, or to arbitrarily transfer the individual to satisfy the objections of the majority of the group.

Poor working conditions still remain a primary source of job dissatisfaction, and this has resulted in a major change in industrial architecture. Henry Ford would be astonished to see the changes in environment wrought in today's factory. While the advent of OSHA (Occupational Safety and Health Administration) certainly contributed to greater attention being paid to safety, noise, light and air enhancement activities in business, industry, and government, this was almost mandatory if those organizations were to be successful in their recruitment of qualified personnel. People simply will not spend one third of their lives in unpleasant and unhealthy surroundings if they can avoid it.

Increasingly, management is delegating authority to employees to determine which enhancements to their working environment should be implemented. The clash between the conceptualizations of industrial architects and designers, safety engineers, managers, employees, and the community, have often resulted in strange compromises, but generally higher morale. Rather than stark white walls and neutral carpeting and upholstery, work areas have often turned into a riot of color, with mixed opinions from the participants, but a much greater affinity for the results than that generally achieved by broad management fiat.

An essential part of the design of any library today is the process of gathering information from the staff regarding their needs in terms of workspace, lighting, furnishing, and equipment. Fifty years ago that was a decision reserved for the architect and administration of the institution. The trend toward open and flexible design in library construction is the direct result of the importance working conditions have upon job satisfaction.

Strangely enough, poor salaries are not a major cause for job dissatisfaction. That may be due in part to the expectation that governance and management will ensure that salaries are kept competitive. Whether that expectation is realized is open to question in the library sector. Recent surveys among the professions and other careers reveal that librarians have fallen behind all categories except welfare recipients. As that realization dawns on more individuals in the library profession, there is certain to be growing job dissatisfaction and demands for higher salaries at a time when public opposition to the tax increases required to correct that deficiency is itself on the increase.

The final elements identified as usual contributors to job dissatisfaction are low status and lack of job security. Until recent years, security was generally a strong factor among those who entered the library profession. While industry offered higher financial rewards, government service at least provided some assurance of continuity. That assurance has vanished as more academic, school, and public libraries have found themselves the loser in the fight for a greater share of the tax dollar. And while librarianship never ranked high among the list of professions, it was at least among the respected governmental careers that one could aspire to after graduation. Regretably, even that advantage has been affected by the increasing public criticism and suspicion of government in general.

In summary, the list of factors leading to job dissatisfaction consist of restrictive administrative policy, incompetent supervision, poor interpersonal relationships, poor working conditions, poor salaries, low status, and lack of security. Many of those elements are common in libraries today, and their existence should signal warning to governance and administration alike that unrest is certain to exist.

In this situation, participatory management cannot serve as a substitute. Administrators cannot expect to satisfy the concerns of their staffs for decent pay and working conditions, or secure futures solely by involving employees in decision making. As Herzberg explains, these are essential elements which must be first satisfied before effective motivation and progressive management theories can be applied. Employee participation, however, can certainly help governance and management to face these problems and contribute to their correction. The manager who fails to draw upon these resources is shortsighted indeed.

We have briefly considered in this chapter the trends in management theory that provide the foundation for participatory management. From the time-and-motion study and fragmentation espoused by Frederick Winslow Taylor, to the birth of the human relations movement and its emphasis upon the employee as an individual, through job reform to the factories of Sweden, where the job was reassembled to give more meaning to the individual in the workplace, we can see that we have come full circle in our attitude regarding the nature of work.

That was not caused by any change in the individual but by the demands of business, industry, and government, the advance of technology (which permitted the elimination of many repetitive tasks), and the shift of the economy from an industrial to a service base. It should be evident that as the standard of living has increased, tolerance for boredom and expectations regarding work have altered. In the Great Depression, personnel could be hired for the library who were willing to laboriously remove the advertising pages from magazines prior to binding to ensure a more compact and less-expensive volume. Today, even the lowest entry-level clerks expect some training which will qualify them for advancement, and want the type of responsibility that justifies that role.

We have experienced in American society a steady growth of expectations in the workplace, and progressive institutions have modified their policies to meet those expectations. Whether the future economy will provide the jobs that are needed to keep pace with these expectations cannot be predicted, given the vagaries of economies and national policy. One thing is certain. Good times or bad, Frederick Winslow Taylor's techniques will never be appropriate for management again. There is a clear and continuous trend toward greater partnership in the workplace, and the traditional prerogatives of the supervisor and the employee must change if society is to function effectively and labor strife is to be avoided.

References

1. Dickson, Paul. *The Future of the Workplace*. New York, Weybright and Talley, 1975. p. 1.

2. Herzberg, Frederick. *Motivation.* (Videotape) Cleveland, AMS, Inc., 1976.

3. Ford, Robert N. *Motivation Through the Work Itself.* New York, American Management Association, 1969.

4. McGregor, Douglas. *The Human Side of Enterprise.* New York, Harper and Brothers, 1949.

5. Argyris, Chris. *Integrating the Individual and the Organization.* New York, Wiley and Sons, 1964.

6. Northrup, Bowen. "More Swedish Firms Attempt to 'Enrich' Production-Line Jobs," in *The Wall Street Journal,* October 25, 1974, p. 1.

7. Herzberg, Frederick. *Work and the Nature of Man.* London, Staples Press, 1968.

II WHAT PARTICIPATORY MANAGEMENT MEANS

LIKE THE proverbial elephant to the blind men, participatory management represents many different things, depending upon one's perspective, role and experience. The focus here is upon the definition which is most commonly accepted by those who have studied it and practiced its application. But for purposes of comparison, and to assure better understanding of the term, variant definitions are also reviewed.

One of the most common conceptions is that participatory management means full control of an organization by its employees. There are certainly some examples of employee-owned firms in the United States and in other parts of the world. The popular press carries notices of failing industries which are purchased by their employees, who successfully turn the tide and bring the firms back to profitability by forgoing pay increases and similar sacrifices.

Misconceptions of Participatory Management

An employee-owned firm is not necessarily a firm that practices participatory management. In fact, the employee-owned firm may hire the type of autocratic management that would not be tolerated under anything but crisis situations. Participatory management and ownership are certainly not synonymous, although there is nothing that would prevent that from happening. Many firms today vigorously promote employee stock-purchase plans that ensure employees a greater stake in the profitability of that corporation. The firm may or may not practice participatory management, but policy is generally favorable toward greater employee participation in sharing the risks and rewards of capitalism.

It can be argued that any public, tax-supported institution is actually employee owned, since its employees are taxpayers, and together with the user-public, they have the greatest stake in the operation of the institution. In the case of public libraries, of course, the governance most frequently is through a group of citizens appointed or elected to ensure the effective management of the institution's resources, and generally some mechanisms exist which provide input by staff and management in policy decisions by that board. In academic and school libraries, and especially special libraries, control is more varied, and may tend to be farther from the ultimate end-user and closer to the institutional bureaucracy. By and large, the fact that an institution is tax-supported does not ensure it is more likely to feature participatory management.

While it would be difficult to substantiate whether public or private enterprise have greater tendency to employ participation in management decisions, there are in the private sector more examples to draw upon that have a demonstrable history. Because of the pressures upon private enterprise to improve productivity, and because of the success participatory management has experienced in improving employee initiative and motivation, private enterprise took an early lead in its application, and is maintaining that lead in the face of legal and psychological barriers which may be effectively hindering many public institutions from adopting this technique.

For some, participation merely means that the employee is allowed to contribute to the decision-making process employed by management, with the ultimate power for policy making remaining with that individual or body. To support that concept is the familiar tenet that while management can delegate authority, it can never delegate responsibility. For many theorists, there is no true participation in management unless the full responsibility rests with the employees required to carry out the specific task, and that as long as management retains any prerogatives, democracy does not exist.

In actual practice, neither extreme is possible. No employee can effectively participate in decision making if he or she is denied power over the ultimate methods they will have to employ to carry out the task required. Conversely, no manager can function effectively if all the decisions rest in the hands of employees. Under these latter circumstances, the employee would become self-governing and the role of the manager would vanish entirely.

In some industrial settings, participation is achieved in an indirect or representative fashion through the procedure of electing or placing employees or their delegates on the governing or advisory boards of the company. Yugoslavia practices this technique widely, and workers' councils are commonplace.[1] Boards of directors of many state-owned foreign nations consist of worker representatives. Often this is a transitional technique for an organization. Prior to granting full participation in all aspects of the company, some firms will grant this type of representation.

It is not unusual in libraries to see employee representation take place in the governance of the institution. Academic institutions more commonly practice this, and some public library boards have been known to include representatives of staff associations or unions to participate, more often on an ex-officio basis, in discussion on policy questions.

The most common form of employee participation is the suggestion box. Whether than can be considered true participation depends upon the attitude of management in implementing suggestions which are received. In some firms, management is free to ignore any and all suggestions received, and the existence of this device is often a reminder to the employees of their powerlessness. In some firms, employees are given review over the suggestions and the power to reward contributors and implement recommendations. The degree to which management is required to adhere to recommended changes directly relates to the extent of democracy in that organization. In some instances, only cost-saving measures are implemented, while in others it may extend to planning and policy making.

Contribution of Likert

One of the foremost theorists in the field of participatory management is Rensis Likert, who for 25 years headed the Institute for Social Research at the University of Michigan. Likert believed that true participatory management only existed when the individual employee achieved self actualization. He stated that "to be highly motivated, each member of the organization must feel that the organization's objectives are of significance and that his own particular task contributes in an indispensable manner to the organization's achievement of its objectives. He should see his role as difficult, important and meaningful."[2]

The problem that Likert recognized is that the goals and objectives of the individual employee and the organization may not be the same. To solve that problem, Likert proposed that the role of management was in large measure to modify the goals of the individual employee and the organization sufficiently so they achieve balance.

The classic case Likert used to illustrate his theories involved the employees of a pajama factory, where management introduced different cost reduction changes to four employee test groups. In the first group, the traditional authoritarian method was employed, where the workers were simply instructed by their supervisors to use new methods developed to cut costs. In the second group, the employees were told by their supervisors that competition was threatening the company and steps had to be taken to modify existing techniques. The workers were asked to select some individuals from among their number who could be trained in the new cost-cutting techniques. Those employees who were selected were granted the opportunity to make their own suggestions on the nature of these new methods, most of which were accepted by the supervisors. The third and fourth groups went through the same process as the second, but all the workers were included in the training and suggestions were invited from all the employees in the fourth group.

The results of the test revealed that production actually declined in the first group, where authoritarian changes were imposed by the supervisors and no participation or communication was permitted. While some time in implementing the change in this first group was gained, production declined to a level 10 per cent below original production norms. In the second group, where partial participation occurred, the exact opposite took place. Production rose to a level 10 per cent above output before the change in manufacturing methods. In the third and fourth employee groups production rose by 25 per cent over previous output.

Central to the effectiveness of this experiment, Likert stated, was the authenticity of the employees' participation in the decisions on process changes, and the commitment of management to implement those decisions. If management only asked for the opinion of the employees on procedures management intended to impose, the same level of effectiveness would not have occurred.

Examples in Industry

The degree of involvement in decision making, and the number of employees brought into the process vary considerably in the experience American industry has had with participatory management. One example of this involves McCormick and Company, a spice and tea company which has since diversified into other products.[3] During the Great Depression the company neared bankruptcy under the authoritarian management practices maintained by its founder. Upon his death, his successor, Charles McCormick, developed a system of employee boards which he called multiple management. Boards were established for all the key areas of specialization in the company, including administration, marketing, manufacturing, etc. In addition, there was an employee, or "junior" board which served to advise the Board of Directors.

The membership of the boards rotated every six months. Personnel consisted of fifteen representatives drawn from a range of employee categories by the management of the firm, although usually they came from middle-management groups. Each of the boards was free to take up any issue, exclusive of wages, which is still the prerogative of top management. While the decisions of these boards were not binding upon management, invariably their recommendations were accepted and implemented.

The major portion of the employees of McCormick and Company were not involved in the decision-making process, but they did participate in a profit-sharing program and stock-purchase plan. The company believed that employees could participate indirectly in decision making through interaction with members of the boards which the company established. Nonetheless, the employees did not have direct control over the procedures that were employed in production. Participation in the direction of the company's operation and its goals did, indeed, occur. All of the factors which are indicative of success with this technique are present. Absenteeism is low. Profits and efficiency are high. The firm receives consistently more applications for its vacancies than it can use. But it is clear that participation in decision making and the self-actualization that Likert felt typified the technique did not extend throughout all levels of the organization.

One of the classic examples of participation in American industry is the Lincoln Electric Company, a manufacturer of arc-welding equipment based in Cleveland, Ohio.[4] During the Great Depression the company was faced with failure until its management elected to take a radical departure in employee relations. Employees were told that if the loss could be eliminated, it would pay each employee a bonus in direct proportion to their contribution to the company's effectiveness.

The methods employed at Lincoln gave each employee a greater share of individual job responsibility and flexibility. Rather than breaking down each task and assigning an individual to perform it, the entire process of fabricating an assembly is given to an employee and he or she is held responsible for inspection and quality control. The resulting number of foremen and inspectors at Lincoln is far fewer because of this sense of responsibility. The rewards to the individual employee are also substantially higher. Pay levels at Lincoln are approximately twice as high as industry standards because of the bonus arrangements, which equal 90–100 per cent of employee salary.

As noted previously, pay is not effective as a motivator after a particular level is attained. But in the case at Lincoln, the dramatically higher pay is linked with a sense of responsibility and greater freedom in the structure of work that provides the self-actualization that Likert stresses. Yet, Lincoln does not employ full participatory management. Its employees do not direct the plans and the operations of that firm. No representatives of employee groups sit on its Board of Directors, nor are there advisory panels such as at McCormick and Company. While the employees have the opportunity to participate in a stock-purchase program, and through the bonus system directly benefit in the profits of the company, their role does not extend to the decision-making level at the top of the organization. They are basically given that freedom in their work, and they do function as virtual independent businessmen, but their control over the company is limited.

Again, the company has been extremely successful. Productivity is exceptionally high. Absenteeism is low. Recruiting personnel is no problem because of the freedom and the high pay scales. The company has come to dominate its field through its application of participatory management to some key elements of its operations.

One other variant should also be reviewed to provide some basis for comparison, and that is the Scanlon plan.[5] A number of American industries have adopted this management technique, and because it features some elements of participation, it deserves consideration by any student of the subject. Joseph Scanlon developed this method based on his experience as an accountant, factory worker, and union official. His methods were first tested during the Great Depression when many firms were facing ruin and alternatives had to be found to keep employees working and production moving.

The elements involve a full disclosure of the company's

financial condition to the employees so they are certain there are no hidden reserves. Another element in the plan requires the development of simple but effective measurements of the company's and employee effectiveness. Most frequently in a manufacturing situation this is the production volume, and the employee's output can be identified as a proportion of that volume. Once that is determined, the company must agree to share all profits above a specified level, mutually agreed upon between the employees and management. With the Scanlon plan, this usually amounts to 75 per cent divided among all the workers, including office employees and management, with the balance going to the investors and owners.

Scanlon plan companies usually, but not always, employ a series of advisory committees to consider cost-cutting measures and other savings. The changes are applied when the committees and management agree, and the benefits are distributed to everyone in the company, regardless of who introduced the suggestion. Generally, wherever the plan has been implemented it has been successful in reducing costs, improving efficiency, and increasing profits to the mutual benefit of the owners, the employees, and management.

Fred Lesieur, who has become the heir to Scanlon, attributes the success of this method to the reality of employee participation. The worker is not given the role of advising the manager or owner. In fact, he is directly participating in the management of the operation and receiving financial rewards for his effort. It is true that the major incentive to the worker under this plan is greater pay, or in the very worst of conditions, retention of his job; nonetheless, it does allow greater freedom in the workplace, and a system that ensures that the worker realizes the consequences of failure to cooperate with his coworkers and management. It is important to realize that in many Scanlon plan companies the union is a full partner in the profit sharing that takes place.

Elements of Participatory Management

With these examples, several elements can be seen which are requisite for arriving at a working definition of participatory management. First and foremost, there must be a definite participation in decision making. As seen in the several examples, that may not involve all the employees of an organization. It may be achieved on a representational basis, or it may extend only to decision making at the job-performance level. But wherever it is introduced, management must be required to carry out the decision that is reached by the group. If it reserves veto power over the decisions made by the employee group, then management is only providing a sense of participation, or an advisory role, and the difference will be immediately recognized by the workers.

Two issues enter into consideration in further weighing whether employees are genuinely given decision-making power. The first is initiative, and some supervisors may come to believe that the initiative for decisions falls entirely into the hands of the employees under participatory management. While that may be true in some situations, the manager does not and should not abdicate responsibility for decision making under this technique. There has been a reaction among employee groups that whenever management brings a decision to the group for action, it has already determined what that decision should be, and is only seeking approval. That may in fact be true, for it would only be human nature for administrators to reach certain conclusions based upon their knowledge of the problem in hand and their experience in the past. The difference is whether the manager, after presenting the problem and making a recommendation, implements or ignores the decision of the group. If the manager ignores the group decision, then participatory management is only an illusion.

The second issue is the autonomy of the worker. While many of the examples that were cited revealed a relatively high level of worker autonomy, that did not necessarily extend to full freedom in the workplace. Certain parameters had to be established in each of those instances to ensure that the action of one employee did not adversely affect other workers or the organization. An employee who decides to report to work at 10 a.m. each morning rather than the customary 8 a.m. could throw a heavier work burden upon coworkers. No one should construe participatory management as a process which allows workers to do whatever they wish. There are constraints which must be established, and if these are arrived at cooperatively between the employee or employee group and management, then this still represents participation and grants the individual employee much greater autonomy than under traditional methods.

These two issues lead to the question of whether true participatory management can occur unless the employees hire or select their own supervisor. In the collegial setting the department head is elected from the faculty of that department or hired from outside by the faculty. However, none of the examples which we have considered in this chapter employed that as an element in its use of participatory management. As noted, the supervisor does have a responsibility and role under this method. He or she does play an important role in the initiation of the decision-making process. In any group process, someone must organize the agenda and coordinate the operations of the group. There is no evidence which would indicate that individuals who perform those functions are any more effective when they are selected by an outside individual or group, such as the owner of a plant, or selected by the group itself.

Because the organization that commits itself to participatory management must ensure participation by all the stakeholders, it is reasonable to assume that in the instance of a library, the governance of that institution would select and hire its own representative to serve as the management. Just as logically, the employees should have the power to select and hire, if necessary, its representatives. In the instance of a private firm, owned by its employees, there would be logic to those employees selecting and hiring their own management. But in the instance where a public institution, governed by an elected or appointed body, had no power to employ its management representatives, then it would be powerless and be unable to function, and the public would be poorly served.

A second necessary element to participatory management is economic return. Here is where problems begin to arise in the implementation of participatory management in the public sector. As evident in the examples cited, all of the organizations coupled decision making with financial incentives in an effort to improve the efficiency of the organization. If the workers in a Scanlon plan company elected to work only two days a week, then the economic results would be the collapse of the company and their loss of employment.

If economic return were up to the management of a company which claimed it practiced participatory management, then the employees could clearly see that the results of their labor would have little impact upon their pay. There must be a guarantee that improved efficiency, greater productivity, reduced absenteeism and cooperation with management and coworkers will result in tangible improvements in pay, or the employee will not truly be participating. It can be argued that management could demonstrate how greater productivity can be converted into lower costs and a salary increase. But as long as the decision regarding who and how much rests in the hands of management, rather than begin shared with the employee, the organization is not adopting all the rules for the application of this technique, and it will not be effective.

There are no public institutions that employ Scanlon plan techniques, for the obvious reason that no profits exist to divide among the employees and management. Nonetheless, it is possible to establish methods which would provide economic return as a component of participatory management in the public sector. We shall examine some of those alternatives and some examples in later chapters. Government agencies can and do accomplish improvements in their operations through various management methods which do not usually employ financial incentives. Many are prevented from employing the incentives developed by business and industry because of civil-service regulations and other legal restrictions designed to prevent favoritism and political influence. Nonetheless, there are methods which can be adopted to promote greater involvement and commitment which are not susceptible to those hazards.

A third factor essential to participatory management is the sharing of management information with all the employees of an organization. Common to the examples cited in this chapter was the access the employee had to financial data and other factors commonplace to management, but normally not distributed to employees. If the employees believe that management is reserving certain information, then distrust will continue.

Employees who are unaware of a library's financial condition may be unwilling to moderate their demands for increased wages or improved working conditions because they have no insight into the impact these costs will have on the institution. Their assumption has to be that the institution has hidden reserves which can be marshalled to help them satisfy their immediate needs. Employees who waste resources or allow facilities to deteriorate do so in ignorance of the effect such action will have on the institution's budget. The relationship between these problems and finance is also known usually only by management.

The budget process is the most common information-sharing opportunity. Those institutions which start this process at the bottom, requesting changes and recommendations from the very lowest unit in the organization, have the best opportunity to demonstrate why priorities must be set. Invariably, when information on why requests have to be reduced and why other requests are granted is not shared with employees, this lack of feedback is deeply resented.

Under participatory management, budgetary requests are generated and shared among the employee units, and they in turn are involved in the decision-making process that determines which requests are honored and which are rejected. A branch librarian might be willing to forego recarpeting at her agency if she is aware that the funds are required to replace the leaky roof at another branch.

If involvement in decision making is essential to participatory management, it is meaningless unless the information necessary for making a sound decision is provided. Many institutions contend that they provide adequate means for communication, but these may not be utilized by employees. The usual vehicle is a newsletter or other house organ. But as long as it is controlled and edited by management, rather than the employees, it will not be an effective tool for facilitating communication and sharing critical management information. If management can exercise veto power over what appears in the house organ, then the typical employee cannot be certain that the facts received are complete or merely selected to serve the need of management. Anyone who has ever examined the house organ and the union newsletter of any organization can easily observe the different perspectives from which management information is viewed.

One problem in satisfying this essential element of participatory management is that when management information is supplied to employees, those employees may not be capable of interpreting it effectively as a basis for decision making. That should not be considered derogatory to the employees, or justify bypassing them. Rather, it demonstrates another role that management has in the participatory technique. Training for decision making has long been a feature in the development of supervisors. They are introduced to evaluative tools and given opportunity to witness the impact that decisions will have upon outcome. For this reason, in any procedure involving employees and supervisors, the managers are always better prepared and informed.

Several alternatives have been used to compensate for this disparity. The first is to devote more time to train all employees in understanding management information, whether that may be financial or statistical. The staff at a branch library with fewer personnel but higher circulation and reference statistics might be less willing to tolerate the featherbedding at a less used but more heavily staffed agency if it could interpret the statistics that management collected.

A second alternative would be for the employees to select from among themselves individuals who could be more thoroughly trained and briefed in the interpretation of information. In larger organizations, this becomes the most practical alternative. It does not mean that management no longer has to keep its employees informed; that must continue. But the fewer number of representatives allows more time to be devoted to ensuring that they have the understanding necessary to specialize and arrive at better informed decisions on behalf of their colleagues.

A third alternative would be to allow the employees to draw

expert assistance from an outside source to help guide them in decision making. In those institutions where unions exist, the paid staff of the union often includes specialists who are able to perform this function. In other situations, consultants may provide the expertise and represent the employees' interests. While this is cumbersome and the third party may not be as closely aware of the organization's problems and the employees' concerns, it does provide a viable alternative when management analysis requires technical or administrative expertise which can not be readily found among the employees or remedied by training through management.

While we generally take it for granted, each employee involved in participatory management must be assured of certain basic rights. Those are the right to speak, the right to due process, and the right to protection from retribution by either management or his fellow workers in the event participation in the process should prove unpopular. Because we have a Bill of Rights, we tend to take these conditions as a given element in this technique. In fact, the Bill of Rights is not assured at the workplace. An individual can be discharged for a variety of reasons, and have no defense in court short of claiming discrimination or violation of a labor contract.

Under more traditional management techniques, the employee can be free to voice his opinion on a decision with the knowledge that since his supervisor reserves the final decision for himself, there is likely to be little impact or influence from the outcome. When democratization occurs, that situation is entirely different, and employees are much more likely to express their true feelings, since they know their views will matter in the outcome. If the supervisor has a fragile ego, retribution can occur in numerous ways, subtle or direct. Ensuring that the employee has an adequate defense is central to participatory management. It does little good to grant employees a part in decision making only to see them suffer ill consequences when that right is practiced.

When democratization occurs, there is also a possibility that traditional procedures protecting due process or grievances may be removed. Employees who traditionally protected individuals who were habitually tardy might be less inclined to do so when they realized the additional burdens placed upon them. They might press for termination in an effort to get a more reliable contributor to the joint work effort.

Another concern is continuity of rights which are earned through democratization. Under standard management procedures, a great deal depends upon the individual management style of the supervisor. If he or she tended to share or delegate decision making with the staff, and established certain flexible policies governing work assignments, all could be lost when that supervisor leaves and is replaced with an individual who practised a more authoritarian style.

To protect the employees in any democratization there should be written guarantees, that practices which are mutually agreed upon between management and the employees are not arbitrarily eliminated when a change in personnel takes place or administrations change. Those policies and procedures should become part of the organization, adopted by its governance. While no policy should ever become fixed to the degree that conditions do not allow modification, there must be a sense of security to the employees that the rules will not change, and some guidelines to management so that consistency and continuity are maintained.

A fifth element essential to participatory management is the right of the individual employees to appeal to some independent judiciary actions taken against them by their supervisor. Without this right, all the other gains and protections are of limited value. Employees must know that they can take decisions reached against them to some independent tribunal for an unbiased opinion that might reverse the action of the supervisor.

In some companies, this may consist of a panel of the employee's peers. They will hear the complaint of the supervisor and the response by the employee and arrive at a binding decision. While the immediate impression might be that the peer group would be biased, and would be unlikely to vote in favor of sustaining the supervisor's decision, under participatory management that is not often the case. The supervisor's action is often taken to protect and further the institution, and since the employees are participating in the operation of that institution, they are often inclined to support the supervisor. Furthermore, the manager would be enforcing policies developed by the employees through the participative method.

A more common method would allow the employee to carry an appeal to a joint committee composed of representatives from management and the workers. This is the customary union model, and there is sufficient evidence to support this as an unbiased judiciary able to weigh the action taken by the supervisor against the employee's position.

A third alternative would be to employ an outside or neutral third party such as an independent arbitrator or a governmental agency established for this purpose. This fact finder might require more time to become familiar with the policies of the organization in order to compensate for any deficiencies in the presentation by either party, but there could be little doubt regarding the fairness of the decision.

In conclusion, the elements which are essential for participatory management are participation in decision making, economic return, access to management information, protection of individual rights, and assurance of the right to appeal to an independent body. Those elements should provide the basis for definition, and are generally accepted by those who have studied and practiced this technique. It can be observed from the examples contained in this chapter that not all of these elements appear in the experiments described. The concerns of governance or management, legal barriers, or the attitude of the employees have often resulted in one or more of the essential components of participatory management being omitted. In practice, there are few examples of true participatory management which can serve as the model. Nonetheless, the technique has proven effective even when limitations have been imposed.

Participatory management is a process in which all or a representative group of employees and management share in the decision making and economic return resulting from that cooperation, and where the employee is protected from arbitrary disciplinary action by his supervisor and his coworkers. Ownership of the organization may or may not be in the hands of the employees, and is not critical to the success of this technique. While this definition may not satisfy all requirements and include all the variants that exist, it should provide a solid foundation for a discussion of its application in coming chapters.

References

1. Jenkins, David. *Job Power: Blue and White Collar Democracy.* Garden City, N.Y., Doubleday and Company, 1973.

2. Likert, Rensis. *New Patterns of Management.* New York, McGraw-Hill, 1961. p. 103.

3. McCormick, Charles P. *The Power of People.* New York, Harper and Brothers, 1949.

4. Lincoln, James F. *Incentive Management.* Cleveland, The Lincoln Electric Company, 1951.

5. Lesieur, Frederick G. *The Scanlon Plan.* Cambridge, Mass., M.I.T. Press, 1958.

III LIBRARY APPLICATIONS OF PARTICIPATORY MANAGEMENT

THERE IS a considerable disparity between those library administrators who state that they practice participatory management and those who actually implement it. In large measure this is due to a general lack of understanding regarding what the techniques are, and either inability or reluctance to implement them. There are many administrators who more correctly indicate they practice a participatory style in their leadership, which frequently means that they allow some input into the decision-making process and may actually delegate some decision making. There are relatively few institutions that have gone to the extent of vesting all decision making in the hands of the staff, none that share the economic return, many that readily share management information, and a considerable number of institutions that have taken positive steps to protect employee rights and grant appeal of disciplinary actions to an independent entity.

Examples in Libraries

Academic libraries have taken a leadership role in the field of participatory management, undoubtedly influenced by the collegial model and by the nature of their staffs. Maurice Marchant provided an excellent overview of the introduction and development of this technique in *Participative Manage-*

ment in Academic Libraries.[1] John Harvey and Mary Parr provided insight into the techniques and results university libraries have obtained from the application of participatory management in the search and screening of applicants for positions.[2]

There have also been various articles on the impact of participatory trends upon academic libraries. Kenneth Shaffer has concluded that the administrator is becoming increasingly more of a chief negotiator because of this trend, coupled with the influence of labor unions, government regulation, and interaction with other units of government.[3] Jane Flener also reviewed the climate of participation in the context of a large university library.[4] George Lewis examined the organizational structures for professional staff participation in decision making at selected universities in the southeastern region of the U.S.[5] Twenty-two library directors and 192 professional librarians responded to this questionnaire to assess the perceived degree of participation at those institutions, the quality of the applications, and their effectiveness. He determined that librarians favored this technique far more than the directors. However, the directors considered themselves far more participative than their staff, although all were uniform in their endorsement of maximizing staff input prior to decision making. In the context of Lewis' definition of participation, neither group strongly favored true participatory management.

In Lewis' study, few of the professional staff believed they were involved to any meaningful extent in the development of library policies and practices. Librarians newly recruited to these institutions and minorities expressed strong desire for greater future involvement. Both the directors and the professional librarians who responded to the questionnaire expressed support for the principle of equal salaries for administrators and nonadministrative personnel with equal credentials, and they believed that greater participation resulted in greater job satisfaction and improved performance.

Charles Lowry reported on a proposed reorganization of the Library at the University of North Carolina at Charlotte which would use the collegial model.[6] Two departments would be established, one for public services and the second for technical services. In each department the "faculty" would operate on a committee basis using participatory management principles and including the clerical employees. An experimental and analysis period would be allowed, with staff members from those departments serving as coordinators, rather than utilizing present administrative personnel. Training sessions were proposed to prepare personnel for management under the new system.

Lowry also completed a thesis which compared the ACRL (Association of College and Research Libraries) standards with the personnel systems of five major universities to determine the degree of involvement with participatory management, among other concerns.[7] The institutions studied were Texas A&M, Harvard, Minnesota, Oklahoma and UCLA. The study concluded that all of those institutions were strongly committed to gaining faculty status for their professional librarians, and that some aspects of participatory techniques were being employed at some of the institutions. The degree of commitment to that technique, however, exhibited considerable variety.

Jerome Yavarkovsky and Warren Haas reviewed the work that was undertaken to improve performance at the Columbia University libraries, through the assistance of a management consulting firm.[8] The major technique adopted was greater participation in both the planning for this change and in the actual operation of the library upon the completion of the reorganization. The change included recasting the staff composition and deployment patterns which emphasized functional relationships and took greater advantage of the subject and operational specialties among the staff. The recommendations of the management firm were thoroughly reviewed by the staff at all levels, and opportunities were provided for staff amendment. To implement the plan, three task forces were established to flesh out the proposal, concentrating upon organization, staffing, and operations. The result was a fully documented organization with each operating unit and position fully defined, and a program accounting budget.

Jane Flener presented a paper to IFLA (International Federation of Library Associations and Institutions) which covered participatory management, among other newer personnel techniques, in terms of their benefits to employees.[9] She noted that the rapid growth of university libraries in recent years required major changes in their administration, including the re-evaluation of their personnel procedures and policies. These changes were brought about through government policies such as fair employment practices, equal employment opportunities, affirmative action, and the growing demands of employees to play a greater role in determining policy at their institutions. Noting that many libraries have adopted management practices developed by business and industry in an effort to improve efficiency, productivity, and to reduce costs, she also reflected on how this has provided greater participation for employees. She reported the steps taken at Cornell, Columbia and the University of California libraries at Berkeley and Los Angeles, as well as the Library of Congress, to involve more staff in the decisions affecting their jobs and providing them with the opportunity to gain growth within the overall goals of the library.

William McGrath has reported on the use of participatory techniques in the development of a long-range strategic plan for the Cornell University Libraries.[10] With the technical expertise of the American Management Association, this institution designed a plan containing alternative strategies to cope with future problems, utilizing the participative model for the purpose.

Paul Cliche described one of the few public-library experiences with participation in his report on the Montreal Citizens Movement project.[11] This organization became alarmed at what it perceived as neglect of the public-library system in that city's administration. To correct that problem, the organization launched an effort to reorganize the governance and administration of the libraries, placing them under the decentralized control of local citizens councils. These councils would participate in the actual administration of the agencies in each section of the city, with the belief that the agencies could be made more responsive to community need.

Dennis Dickinson has provided some precautions.[12] Noting

that the participatory technique is often considered a panacea for all types of problems facing libraries, he cautioned that many enthusiasts fail to understand and define its application properly, and proceed on the basis of unwarranted assumptions. He also expressed concern about the fragmentation which occurs because of the subsequent delegation of authority among different levels of an institution. He warned that many advocate the technique but few understand where it will lead, and may be unprepared for the consequences.

Victoria Musman reported on a study undertaken among five small California public libraries designed to provide information about management style in those institutions.[13] A majority of the directors of those institutions perceived that they employed a participatory style of management. All of the professional staffs of those institutions were polled regarding their perceptions, which revealed a different conclusion.

In an effort to determine whether the Act of Participation passed in Sweden had any impact upon Swedish libraries, Inger Fredriksson surveyed the staffs of 23 libraries in the Stockholm region.[14] This act provided personnel in Swedish institutions with certain rights, including periodic staff meetings, house journals to communicate their concerns, access to management information, and an increased role in decision making for their institution. The questionnaire also sought to determine the degree of participation in development of book-selection policies by the staff, who contributed to the staff journals and the criteria for selection of staff for various training courses. The results of the survey indicated that few libraries had fully implemented the provisions of the act.

Reasons for Limited Application in Libraries

There most certainly have been other experiences with participatory techniques in libraries which have not been reported in the journals, and almost everyone can recall some institution in which they may have directed or worked where some elements of this management method were used or tested. But

I believe it would be safe to report that it has not been applied in its truest form in many institutions. There are several logical reasons for its limited application among libraries.

Foremost among the barriers to its adoption among libraries in the uncertainty that the technique will achieve results similar to those in private industry. There have been few if any empirical tests of participatory management in libraries to verify that it would improve service, lower costs, and enhance staff attitude and performance. Much has been written about expectations envisioned by the application of this method, and some libraries have written about their use of some elements of the process, but few can provide hard evidence that staff participation can accomplish in libraries what it has for industry. Even among the theorists, there is some evidence that the results obtained from the industrial applications may be more the results of the "Hawthorne" effect than from greater democratization. Critics can also point out that the introduction of these techniques in foreign countries hasn't radically improved productivity, or even changed the attitude of the worker. In short, while the trend may be clearly toward giving the worker a greater voice in the future of an institution, there is little to confirm conclusively that this method will do anything more for the organization than the traditional techniques.

Attitude is another barrier. If the library director is not impressed with participatory management, and feels uncomfortable in its application, there is not much hope that the institution will adopt it unless the director is forced into its introduction by either governance or staff. Even in that situation, the attitude of the chief executive will be critical to its success. If the manager fails to delegate decision-making prerogatives or fails to supply the management information needed, the experience is certain to be disappointing to all.

It has been determined that those administrators most likely to support democratization are those possessing a strong sense of achievement, self reliance, and confidence in the ability of others.[15] They tend to be receptive to new ideas, self-critical, and possess good ability to compromise. They are sensitive to the needs of others and possess strong organizational capability. With those attributes, administrators should have every likelihood of success even if they do not adopt participatory management. Nonetheless, it does reveal that the weaker administrator, who would most benefit from this technique, and whose institution would be most in need of its adoption, would be least likely to use it. Insecure managers are not likely to divest themselves of the power they hold over other employees.

But attitude is not only a barrier for the manager. Many employees might be equally reluctant to accept greater responsibility. Paul Bernstein notes in *Workplace Democratization* that the method is opposed among employee groups in several nations because of their long cultural reliance upon authority figures.[16] He cites one example where turnover actually increased in a Latin American nation after an American firm introduced participation because the employees felt that if management was asking them for their advice and recommendation on key decisions, the firm would soon be out of business.

Historically, the professional librarian has not been a militant employee. While the stereotype has changed substantially in recent years, there are still many librarians who believe they are "professionals" and above labor and management issues such as greater democratization in the workplace. Some library administrators report much greater militancy in their clerical and paraprofessional staff than among professionals. Curiously, when many library administrators review the steps they have taken to democraticize their institution, they refer only to what has been done in concert with the professional staff. Groups such as clerical, paraprofessional, and maintenance personnel, who have greater cause for grievance, are often ignored in the process.

In many instances of democratization, there are employees who remain outside the participating group. They are interested in putting in their day's work, receiving fair pay, and going home for the night or weekend without the troubles and tribulations of their institution upon their shoulders. A greater role in decision making for their institution is the last thing they want, and there are often enough individuals possessing this attitude in an organization to hamper introduction of this technique. Even a grudging acceptance of participatory practices is no certainty progress will occur. There has to be mutual interest in participation in decision making in the organization. Both management and staff must believe greater democratization will improve the library and working conditions, or the method is certain to stumble.

There is also the valid concern that democratization may result in perceived or real regression in institutional policies. One director informed me of his disappointment with participatory management over the issue of affirmative action. With the approval of his board, and the reluctant participation of his staff, he had successfully implemented a progressive affirmative action plan for his institution which was designed to correct very real deficiencies in the racial balance of the staff. Considerable training and time was devoted gaining the support and understanding of the staff.

Feeling after a year had passed that some genuine progress had occurred, the library director began to introduce a greater level of participation into decision making on policies and procedures. One of the first committees established was delegated responsibility for revision of personnel policies, and following training and familiarization, the director looked forward to some progressive change and honest evaluation of existing personnel policies and practices. Instead, the first thing the staff committee did was to introduce elimination of the affirmative action plan so painstakingly introduced the previous year. Staff felt so threatened by it that they established policies which would compound the racial imbalance existent at that institution. Further changes were introduced that only solidified the position of those members of the staff most reluctant to liberalize personnel policy, including the adoption of repressive dress codes and harsher penalties for infractions of rules.

It is axiomatic that personnel in many institutions, particularly those who have acquired a patina of moss, are not favorable to change. They have valid concerns regarding security and a host of other hard-earned perks and the introduction of radical reform in administration and jobs is certain to be viewed with a jaundiced eye. Dealing with this problem will be the subject of later chapters, but the administrator who introduces participatory management in an institution where the staff is either unprepared or reluctant to accept it is practicing another form of authoritarianism, and the results may be the exact opposite of those intended.

Another barrier to adoption of this technique is likely to be the law or regulations affecting the governance or administration or operation of the institution. While it is safe to state there is little likelihood legislation currently exists which prevents implementation of any management technique, the practical application of participatory management requires greater flexibility than many legislative drafting bureaus may have anticipated.

For example, the powers and duties of most public library boards are contained and are guaranteed in state statutes. Invariably those powers include policy making, budgeting, approval of personnel and a host of other elements dear and near to the hearts of any devotee of participatory management. While it is true many of these powers are regularly delegated by governance to management, it is cold comfort to any employee group to realize that the opportunity to participate in decision making has been granted by management, subject to review and approval by trustees. Further, even if governance does grant direct authority and power to use these prerogatives, that delegation could end with a change in administration. Only a revision in state legislation would assure employees that their rights could be maintained, and there would be little likelihood of that occuring, given the threat this would create for other library boards. Even the existence of a written contract between governance and the employees would not provide assurance their rights could be retained, for no board could legally commit future boards to a delegation of powers which are legally vested to that body.

There are other regulatory and administrative barriers to greater democratization, which are surmountable, but cumulatively they may mitigate against radical change. For example, most public library directors are accountable to their city finance officials for the budgeting and allocation of funds Delegation of this responsibility to a staff committee could leave that committee with the assumption it has power over those elements, when in fact this is a responsibility which is shared between the city and the library. The finance officials might be faced at budget time with a group of employees ill prepared to justify the changes they propose in the budget, with the risk that the appropriation might be reduced. Granted, the library's finance department could provide the staff committee with the tools necessary to handle this challenge, but they may be jealous of their lost prerogatives and anxious for the technique to fail.

Yet another example of the regulatory barriers that could exist to implementation of this method is civil service, a factor affecting many libraries. One of the basic tenets of civil service is job classification with a fairly specific enumeration of duties and responsibilities. Under participatory management, effort is undertaken to grant greater responsibility and flexibility in the job. While this can often be achieved with the cooperation and understanding of receptive civil-service officials, upgrading salaries to compensate the employee for broader job requirements and increased responsibilities may be more difficult, given the similarity of that job title in other institutions which have more rigid interpretations of the job. Then there is the complication caused when the position becomes vacant. Participatory management involves almost the custom redesigning of jobs to fit the individual goals, abilities, and aspirations of the incumbent. When that person leaves, the position might change drastically if it is filled from a civil-service list.

The financial implications of participatory management present yet another barrier to its adoption. Nothing has been written on what an institution adopting this technique may expect in terms of finances to support the conversion and to maintain the process over the long run. As previously noted, to be effective the employees will require extensive training in the techniques and in various aspects of the institution's operations which will be completely alien to them. If that training is inadequate, then it can be expected that the institution will pay the consequences in poor decisions based on inadequate familiarity with the methods, procedures, and problems of the activity.

Communications are also critical to the success of participatory management, and the cost of providing the employees with additional avenues of expressing their concerns, or sharing information about their problems and progress, can be considerable when the preparation of the copy, its editing, printing, and distribution is considered. In a medium-sized library that could represent a commitment of over $20,000 per year, and the figure could be considerably higher depending upon the size of the institution, the nature of the publication, and the frequency of its distribution. The Chicago Public Library spends an estimated $24,000 per year to prepare, print, and distribute a simple monthly newsletter to its 2,000 employees.

There is also the cost involved with the dissemination of management information for the employees of the institution. Reproduction and distribution of budget documents, financial and statistical reports, policy drafts, personnel reports, and general memoranda which might be of value (but which might inundate departments with tremendous amounts of paper) could create worse management and personnel problems than the absence of the documents.

There is also the time which the employees and management must commit to decision making. The greater the number of individuals involved, and the broader the representation required, the greater will be the time required to reach a decision. While it can be argued that the decision is more likely to be the correct one, because of the greater input, it is also likely to be costly. No one can place a dollar value on the cost and benefits of employee participation in decision making, because the extent of that involvement is impossible to foresee. But that does add greater uncertainty to the advantages of the method.

It has been hypothesized that while some additional expense will occur, that will be quickly offset by improved attendance, reduced turnover, lower costs, and increased productivity. A study undertaken by the Indianapolis-Marion County Public Library in Indiana revealed, however, that this institution's turnover and absenteeism rates were no better or no worse than a broad sampling of businesses, industries, and governmental institutions, despite a relatively low salary rate compared with those organizations, and despite the adoption of a participative style of management at the Library.[17]

A similar study was undertaken by the Chicago Public Library to determine if its personnel turnover and absenteeism supported that earlier study.[18] While neither study proves or disproves the fact that participatory management can improve attendance and lower turnover, any administrator should examine the local rates of business, industry and government, before using this as a justification for adopting participatory management.

Another element which libraries lack as an incentive to control costs is the profit margin. As noted previously, economic return to the employees is a certain incentive to them to improve productivity and lower cost. A high percentage of time devoted to decision making and considerable expense in communication and sharing of management information will drive costs up and reduce economic return to the employees. Because libraries do not have a profit which can be distributed to its workers, at least not in its truest sense, there is no controlling factor which would keep in balance the costs of implementing participatory management. Staff could devote endless amounts of time to decision making, or commit inordinate amounts of the institution's budget to communication devices.

Another uncertainty with the adoption of this management technique is the impact upon networking, and multitype, interlibrary cooperation. The philosophical foundation for networking and cooperation is that resources are finite, and if certain costs can be shared, the benefits to all the participants will increase. But like stone soup, there are certain commitments which the participants will have to make, or the cooperative concept will fail. Each institution must contribute, or the soup will remain nothing but water and stone.

Professionally, all libraries support the concept of networking and cooperation. However, when decisions are made regarding the allocation of resources in an institution, there is certain to be a shortage to satisfy expressed needs. There may be a greater tendency to satisfy internal needs rather than those which contribute toward broad professional goals. It has been observed that support for networks and multitype, interlibrary cooperation is a concept supported more in thought and word than in deed, and that the principle support for this rests with the chief executives of most libraries, rather than representing a strong commitment among the rank and file.

The greatest uncertainty in the adoption of participatory management, however, is not knowing where it will lead. For many administrators there is a deep unexpressed fear that once decision making and authority is shared, the employees and governance will conclude that there is no longer a real need for a chief executive. Taken to its logical end, participatory management should arrive at the point where all employees are self-directed, and the various committees and boards will eliminate the need for any coordinative role.

Lest that be sufficient to cause supervisors reading this book to close their minds to the prospect of greater democratization, let me hasten to point out that no institution which has adopted the technique has found it practical or feasible to dismiss its administrative staff. There are certainly changes which are required for any manager, just as there are for the employee, and these will be discussed in later chapters. A metamorphosis must take place and there are risks which any manager must accept if they elect to employ this method, but there are tangible benefits.

There is also the possibility that democratization could lead to stagnation for both the organization and its workforce. The thrust of this technique is toward greater efficiency and higher return for its employees. Traditionally, it has been management or governance that has advocated research and development, and committed the resources of the organization toward the development of new products or services which were essential to keeping the institution viable and competitive. What happens then when the decision on the allocation of slender resources is placed in the hands of employees who might be more motivated by increasing their economic return? Does the institution stay with a tried and true service or product rather than taking the risk to enter a new field? The experience in industry has been that the company continues to evolve, and that employees involved in the decision-making process recognize that a certain degree of risk-taking is essential if the company is to hold its position in the marketplace.

But what would be the tendency in the public sector, where there is no necessity to maintain a strong and aggressive position in the marketplace? There is no experience on which to base conclusions. It could be possible that the employee committee weighing the usually heavy set of requests at budget time might allocate funds to establish a new collection in anticipation of changes in the curriculum, or commit staff and materials to serve the Spanish-speaking community that has grown up overnight near one of the public library branches. On the other hand, if the participants are all stakeholders in the library, there might be a greater tendency, once again, to satisfy existing internal needs before commitment is made to establishment of any new programs or services.

In a public institution there are, however, countervailing pressures through governance and users which might ensure that the institution will continue to evolve and remain responsive to its clientele. Administrators have continuously been faced with the unpleasant decision of cutting the quality of existing services and programs when they could not gain additional support from their financing sources for development and reserach necessary to satisfy need requirements. The result of this has been steady and gradual erosion of all libraries, with these institutions becoming less able to maintain existing services, while they are also less capable of playing a meaningful role in satisfying emerging new requirements. Perhaps a decision by the employees of the institution to maintain existing services and a demand that the funding authority commit adequate resources for the newer responsibility might be a more realistic method to cope with the dilemma. Coupled with the support and understanding of the affected clientele, the funding authority might find itself in the position of having to react positively, rather than refusing the request of the administrator as it was accustomed to doing over past years.

In this chapter, we have reviewed some library experiences with participatory management and seen that there has been little application of this technique in its truest form. Where it has been introduced, it has been primarily as an administrative style, with some sharing of responsibility for decision making by staff. Compared with the private sector, there has been greater conservatism to adoption of democratization. Exception to this would be in the academic field, where they have been more greatly influenced by the prevailing faculty model in colleges and universities.

We have considered some of the problems or barriers to the adoption of participatory management, basically attitudinal on the part of both management and employees, legal and regulatory, financial, and a host of uncertainties based on lack of experience in the application of this method. In the forthcoming chapter, we shall discuss some of the more positive aspects, or reasons why there are tangible and practical benefits to its use. There are definitely some problems in the democratization of the workplace, and any manager must be aware of the limitations of the technique. It cannot solve the problems of every organization, or satisfy the needs of every employee or manager. It is a tool which only has utility if its users know when it can benefit them and their organization, and how it can be used. That is what we shall turn to next.

References

1. Marchant, Maurice P. *Participative Management in Academic Libraries.* Westport, Conn., Greenwood Press, 1976.

2. Harvey, John F., and Mary Parr. "University Library Search and Screen Committees," *College and Research Libraries,* July 1976, p. 347-55.

3. Shaffer, Kenneth R. "The Library Administrator as Negotiator: Exit the 'Boss,'" *Library Journal,* September 1, 1975, p. 1475-80.

4. Flener, Jane G. "Staff Participation in Management in Large University Libraries," *College and Research Libraries,* July 1973, p. 275-79.

5. Lewis, George R. *Professional Staff Participation in the Decision-Making Process in Selected University Libraries.* Washington, D.C., EDRS, 1975.

6. Lowry, Charles, and others. *Proposed Library Reorganization.* Charlotte, N.C., North Carolina University, J. Murray Atkins Library, 1975.

7. Lowry, Charles B. *The ACRL Standards and Library Governance, a Comparison of the Personnel Systems of Five Major Academic Libraries.* (Thesis) Chapel Hill, N.C., University of North Carolina, School of Library Science, 1974.

8. Yavarkovsky, Jerome, and Hass, Warren J. *The Columbia University Management Program.* Paper Presented at the General Council Meeting of the International Federation of Library Associations, Washington, D.C., November 1974.

9. Flener, Jane G. *Newer Approaches to Personnel Management.* Paper Presented at the General Council Meeting of the International Federation of Library Associations, Washington, D.C., November 1974.

10. McGrath, William E. *Development of a Long Range Strategic Plan for a University Library: The Cornell Experience: Chronicle and Evaluation of the First Year's Effort.* Ithaca, N.Y., Cornell University, University Libraries, 1973.

11. Cliche, Paul. "The Montreal Citizens Movement Project: Transforming the City Library into a Network of Community Centres Run By Local Citizens," *Argus,* May–August 1978, p. 59–62.

12. Dickinson, Dennis W. "Some Reflections on Participative Management in Libraries," *College and Research Libraries,* July 1978, p. 253–262.

13. Musman, Victoria Kline. "Managerial Style in the Small Public Library," *California Librarian,* July 1978, p. 7–20.

14. Fredriksson, Inger, "Are You Allowed to Join in the Decision Making?," *Biblioteksbladet,* August 1977, p. 133–136.

15. Bernstein, Paul. *Workplace Democratization: Its Internal Dynamics.* Kent, OH, Kent State University Press, Comparative Administration Research Institute, 1976.

16. *Ibid.* p. 5.

17. *Absenteeism and Pay Study.* Indianapolis, IN, Indianapolis-Marion County Public Library, 1979.

18. *Personnel Attendance Report.* Chicago, Chicago Public Library, 1980.

IV WHEN, HOW, AND WHY PARTICIPATORY MANAGEMENT CAN CONTRIBUTE TO YOUR ORGANIZATION

THERE IS a common exercise in many introductory management courses which is worth calling to your attention if you have not practiced it before. It involves a hypothetical camping trip, and the instructor generally asks students to list each of the things they should bring with them. After allowing time for this tabulation, the instructor then directs that individuals confer with someone else in the class to see if there was anything missed, or something that could be left behind to reduce the load. Invariably, you will improve your listing. The instructor will then suggest that you organize in small groups and see if any further changes are appropriate. This process continues, of course, until the entire class is reviewing the list. You have learned the lesson that the greater input you can obtain, the better the results will be.

Changes in Industrial Employment

The United States has gone through enough social change in the past century to keep an army of psychologists, historians, and librarians occupied for the next two thousand years, interpreting, analyzing, collecting, and organizing just the major elements. One hundred years ago, this was a nation of rugged individualists, breaking across the continent, trying to get as much space between us and our fellow human as possible. Industries were founded by individuals, who were somehow able, by grit and perserverance, and perhaps a touch of larceny, to marshall the resources necessary to accomplish miracles. The American public-library movement, in fact, was largely founded and profoundly influenced by the philanthropy of one of those individuals.

We were taught that many of the institutions we respected were really the shadow of one man (or woman), and that all an individual needed to achieve success in this world was forty acres and one mule. Individual rights and individual freedom are what we fought several world wars over. Our literature is haunted by the American fixation on individualism, and biographies still tend to be heavily read sections in any library. Somewhere, however, the individual became more like a myth than a reality. Like the western hero who rode off into the sunset, the image remained in our mind, but we knew his time had passed. Perhaps that occurred during the Great Depression, when no matter how good individuals may have been in their work, they were still let go. The individual was powerless to change the situation, in spite of ability.

But there were other factors at work. If the assembly line was still king, and was to win the war in the 1940's, there were also changes in the complexity of American business, industry, and government. Henry Ford could brag that his Model T could be put back together by any farmboy with a screwdriver and a roll of bailing wire, but it would require a fairly well-educated farmboy possessing far more than a screwdriver and a roll of bailing wire to put a modern automobile together today.

The specialization which began with the industrial age spread to all elements of society, and it required teamwork and painstaking coordination to gather, fit, and implement all of the talent necessary to turn America into the most productive and efficient nation on earth. Whole industries which didn't exist in the 1940's and 1950's were suddenly among the Fortune 500 by the 1960's, and by the 1970's they were becoming trans-national conglomerates. Educational institutions by the tens of thousands were created out of prairie, and libraries began to look at computers and telecommunications for help rather than as competition.

Finding methods which improved the effectiveness of people working together was clearly of critical importance to management in every organization, and it became quickly apparent that the task would not be easy. People had been accustomed to working as individuals for centuries, and while the industrial revolution brought them out of their cottages, they were still considered individual interchangeable parts to be plugged into vacant stretches of the assembly line, like old shirts on a clothes line.

Given this history and the myth of the individual who could accomplish all things, the average worker found the transition difficult. While there was need for enough money to keep food on the table, the individual worker would compromise and put in his day at the mill. He could take comfort in his family, and hope for their future, and perhaps, there might always be some recognition from the boss that could result in promotion or a pay increase.

But, by the 1950's, the average worker was no longer worried about keeping food on the table. He had gone through the Great Depression and won a world war. His nation was now producing as never before, and through his union he was going to get a piece of the rewards from this unparalleled prosperity. He had security, recognition, sufficient salary, and his children were getting a college education.

By the time those children entered the workforce in the 1960's and 1970's, management started discovering that all those carrots and sticks which had evolved over the years since the advent of the industrial revolution where not having any effect. Those children of the average worker, who had endured years of mind-numbing routine in return for a living wage, had no intention of following in their father's footsteps. For the most part, they were starting off at the level their father had reached after forty years in the workplace. They expected a good wage and decent working conditions and progressive fringe-benefit policies. All of the incentives that management had parceled out over the years were now out on the table at the start, and management was suddenly left with a dilemma. It could not increase productivity enough to radically change the pay or the benefits; yet to keep its labor force satisfied, it had to accomplish that or go out of business.

Motivating the Worker

The secret was motivation. If management could somehow motivate the worker to improve his productivity and efficiency, then the enterprise would thrive. For workers, with a decent salary, security, good working conditions, and other basic needs a certainty, the only issues of concern were whether their careers would provide fulfillment, satisfaction, a sense of accomplishment, and a feeling of individual responsibility. And that is where participatory management enters.

Let's start with the U.S. Army. If ever an organization should have a problem with recruiting and motivation, the U.S. Army would rank near the top of the list. It cannot pay a competitive salary, and if there is any doubt about individualism, recall those uniforms. In the Army, one does not march to the beat of a different drummer. If library administrators believe they have personnel problems, they should pause to talk with someone who has served as an officer in this organization. Generally, the personnel they recruit have to be trained to do everything, and there is almost certain turnover, continuously.

Yet even the U.S. Army can change, with the help of various consulting firms. Based on the military example, you can gain a taste of what the world is coming to. If there is anything you have ever wanted to drive or operate in the world, the Army has it. Marketing analysis revealed that what young people want more than anything these days is achievement. That is why you will find plastered on billboards, in television commercials, and in full color magazine advertisements, young men of all colors, shapes and sizes driving tanks, armored vehicles, earth moving equipment, operating radar and preparing helicopters, and neatly in the corner is the invitation to join this fine organization and achieve!

There is something closely associated with achievement, and that is most certainly recognition, and if there is anything the U.S. Army can provide it is recognition for your accomplishments and service. Every recruiting sergeant is a virtual billboard proclaiming this fact, for his entire chest is covered with ribbons and service medals. The Army has always understated this aspect to some degree, at least publicly. But realization that recognition is a major motivator and recruiting tool has brought this organization to shed all inhibitions, and you will be certain to see heroes and heroines appearing in more and more advertising to illustrate the advantage of service to your country.

Industrial psychologists have long realized that advancement is also a key motivator, and here the Army minces few words. One of the most common billboards and posters found in post offices throughout the nation is a picture of a young man and woman with sergeants' stripes on their arms, with the single word "Advancement" underneath.

The military example best illustrates the change in the incentives and motivators management has come to employ to attract and satisfy workers today. An examination of the classified employment section of any major newspaper will underscore that fact. Salaries, fringe benefits and working conditions are not the large type in the corporate ads. Instead, these companies are selling themselves based on intangibles such as "growth," "increased responsibility," and "rapid advancement." Any personnel director can verify that major questions pertain to those issues. It is not simply a case where the young candidate is too shy to inquire about pay or fringe benefits. Those are taken for granted.

Achievement and Recognition

Participatory management provides the most dramatic means for an employee to gain achievement of any of the management techniques ever developed. Under more traditional methods, the only way the employee could become the master of one's own fate was through decades of hard work, eventually becoming a supervisor, or the chief executive, or the owner of the company. Participatory management, however, places him on equal footing with not only coworkers, but with the supervisor, and that is a very gratifying position to be in if you are just out of school and anxious to demonstrate your knowledge and talents.

There is another side to this as well. On an assembly line, the ability to see the actual end result of your effort was denied. You could go out and buy the product, but it was not the same as knowing that you had constructed the vehicle. Participatory management does not let you construct the whole product, but it gives you an opportunity to control some of the decisions that result in that construction, and that is an immense step forward and provides a feeling of achievement.

In the library setting there is an equally good opportunity to see the role that achievement plays in job satisfaction. A classic example involves an acquisitions problem experienced by one large public library. A backlog of orders had developed in the Acquisitions Department, brought about through a loss of personnel and a subsequent budgetary reduction which prevented their replacement. Discussing with the staff of that unit various methods of eliminating the backlog, the director learned that a substantial number of individual branch orders were duplicative. As might be suspected, many of the agencies were ordering the same titles and if there could be some consolidation, the workload upon acquisitions could be considerably reduced.

After discussions with members of his administrative staff, the director elected to initiate an experiment which would allow the library to determine whether centralization of selection for a portion of the branch book budget would allow real gains to be achieved by the Acquisitions Department without adversely impacting the quality of the branch collections or usage. A task force was established consisting of representatives from the branches, collection development, and Acquisitions departments to work out the procedures, establish a control group and a test group, and to construct evaluative techniques.

Almost immediately the project received the strong opposition of branch professional personnel. Even though the procedures provided them with opportunity to continue using the bulk of their book budget for clearly-defined local needs, and they had representatives involved with the project (which further was defined as a test for only a six-month period), they were adamant in their rejection of this alternative to elimination of the backlog in Acquisitions. They preferred to endure the delay in the receipt of new materials rather than suffer the loss of their entire book-selection responsibilities. The test could not proceed with that opposition, and the results were inconclusive.

The major factor which the director failed to consider in dealing with this problem was the adverse impact that centralized selection would have upon the sense of professional achievement. Although it could be proven that as much as 80% of the materials selected by these branches were duplicative, the branch personnel prided themselves on the application of their professional training to the development of these collections, and would not accept an alternative which denied them that sense of achievement.

Subsequent to this, other alternatives were developed which provided means for branches to subscribe to plans which provided new books of a popular type, as well as plans which selected certain broad subject categories in high demand. On that basis the branches elected to commit major portions of their book budget, even though it represented a delegation of their book selection responsibility. The difference was twofold. Even though the branch professional staff accepted centralized selection in this form, it was a voluntary decision on their part, rather than one imposed by an administrator. Second, the staff still had a sense of achievement, since they were making the decision which they recognized would bring the same books to their agency at a more rapid rate.

Participatory management is also unique in the opportunity it provides for individual recognition of employees. More traditional management techniques submerge the individual in the system. The classic story told about this concerns a quality control inspector on an automobile assembly line, who kept on discovering a rattle inside the door of every fourth automobile that passed down the line. Someone consistently dropped small parts, tools, and soft drink bottles inside the door assemblies. After considerable detective work, he finally traced it to an employee who readily admitted the vandalism. He told the inspector that he felt that he did such a good job on his portion of the assembly that "his" cars deserved a special signature, and when the door assemblies were opened to remove the rattle, people would recognize how good his work was.

Large and complex organizations rarely allow individuals to receive recognition for their achievements, and what good is achievement, after all, if no one realizes what you have done but yourself? For this reason one of the major justifications for greater democracy in the workplace is to allow the individual to gain an identity. Administrators who employ participatory techniques often express astonishment at the relatively conservative attitude their employees display when they are placed on task forces or committees requiring decision making. They anticipate the employees will be radical in their approach to various problems because of their demand for participation in management. What they may have been seeking is greater recognition for themselves as individuals and professionals. It is my observation that administrators are usually greater risk takers and tend to be more radical in their approach to problems then their employees, who have to implement those decisions.

In large libraries there is much greater emphasis on task forces or committee work in an effort to provide input as a basis for decision making, as well as to provide a means for individual employees to gain some recognition of their ability and learn from other staff members who have pertinent experience in other departments. Graduate school faculty members often report the reluctance of students to accept appointment to larger libraries because of their fear they will be lost in a large bureaucracy and never gain the recognition important to their career aspirations. Greater use of the task-force technique, and effective utilization of the recommendations coming from these ad hoc administrative units, should correct this problem.

The need for improved communication among employees, which is an essential element in participatory management, is yet another reason why it provides opportunity for recognition among employees. For those who are not involved in a particular task force, but interested in its goals, the awareness that contribution can be made through recognized procedures is extremely helpful. Later in this book there will be a more thorough discussion of the use of task forces in participatory management, but it is essential when such groups are created from among the employees and management, that the employees are aware of who is serving on the task force, and what its goals and objectives are. With good internal communications, employees should be able to communicate their concerns to pertinent members of committees, ensuring the broadest possible input. The results of the task-force effort should also be reported, not only to keep staff and management informed, but to allow some additional recognition for the efforts of the individual contributors.

The work itself represents a prime motivator to most individuals. There are few people in the library profession who enrolled in anticipation of great wealth. They enjoy the work, and that is equally true of most trades and professions. People will endure great discomfort and indignities, poor working conditions, and low salaries if they derive satisfaction from practicing their acquired skills. Traditional management techniques certainly allow employees to exercise their talents, but often hinder them to a greater degree than does the participatory technique.

An artist whose work would be narrowly prescribed by a supervisor, or a metal worker who is told not only what to construct, but how to proceed with construction, will not derive the same level of satisfaction from their work as employees who are granted greater freedom in organizing their own work methods. It may be true that participatory management in its practical application does not allow every worker to do his or her own thing. Parameters must often be established because of the setting. Nonetheless, democratic management permits more flexibility.

The difference between democratic techniques and more traditional means is that employees have a greater voice in determining how they will perform their work. A good example of this is what happened during the automation of a technical-processing department in an older public library. A large backlog existed and the addition of more personnel was not financially possible. A staff committee was introduced to a variety of newer equipment and techniques. Visits were arranged to other libraries employing this equipment, and staff had the opportunity to test many of the devices and talk with personnel who used them.

Following this, a committee of the entire department, composed of management, professional, and clerical staff, determined which equipment they wished to employ, reviewed the specifications, and then aided in the placement of the equipment, after reviewing and finally accepting one of several equipment and furniture layouts. The result was an efficient assembly line, and one of the employees later acknowledged that she never expected to find herself in such a setting. Rather than being demeaning to her, she came to realize how it would help her in her work and contribute to the work of her colleagues as a result of give-and-take on the committee.

The manager of that unit could have imposed that particular work setting upon her staff, but she elected to let the workers made the decisions on what was required. They understood the work and what was needed. The only parameter that was prescribed was the need to establish a more automated technical processing unit so that the backlog could be reduced. In participatory management it is often the role of the supervisor to carefully define the objective and establish any parameters. In this fashion, the employees are fully aware of their role and conflicts are avoided. Both the staff and the supervisor knew that the decision did not involve whether to automate the technical services department or not. Management had established the fact that it could not provide additional personnel to permit the older, manual methods to continue, but it indicated that it could find sufficient resources to acquire more modern equipment for the unit.

Increased Responsibility and Advancement

While the work itself is a powerful motivator, and greater democratization of management methods enhance this, there is a similar advantage to this technique in that it provides increased responsibility for employees. Earlier in this book there was a caution that some employees do not want increased responsibility. While this is true, it is equally true that they may be willing or anxious to assume greater responsibility in work assignments.

The clerk who already has more work than he or she can handle, may not be anxious to accept yet another assignment imposed by the supervisor. Often, a supervisor who observes an employee who is not fully occupied will attempt to change that situation by adding another job assignment. What that supervisor may fail to realize is that the employee is unhappy with the existing assignments or feels incapable of handling them. Another assignment, particularly of a similar nature, may represent only sufficient motivation for the employee to resign.

Increased responsibility can be either a form of recognition or punishment, and the way the work is presented by the supervisor is critical to the attitude the worker will take. In participatory technique, the employee or employee group is typically faced with a problem or task, and they are given the right to decide who is to assume responsibility for it. The employee who accepts responsibility in this setting wins recognition, and is certain to have a more positive attitude about the assignment. If the supervisor is handed the responsibility back by the individual or group, then they are making a conscious decision that it can be delegated as the manager deems appropriate.

In many situations, however, people enjoy the opportunity for increased responsibility. It satisfies their ego, gives them additional experience which will qualify them for advancement, allows personal growth, and grants them a prerogative previously held only by management. Some people may complain about the responsibilities that they have been required to assume, but they usually have the option to reject those duties if they wish. If they assume responsibilities on their own initiative, they will rarely complain, and only when restrictions are imposed upon their exercise of those responsibilities which they feel may hamper their effectiveness.

While no one has reported on whether traditional management methods or participatory techniques allow greater opportunity for personal advancement, it can be safely assumed that more democratic methods have the edge. As previously noted, the latter technique allows opportunity for great achievement, recognition, greater chance to exercise one's work skills, and increased responsibility.

A confidential study conducted by one large urban public library did reveal that those employees who served on a variety of special task forces tended to receive more promotions than a separate group of employees who did not participate.[1] While this may reveal an inherent bias in the sense that the employees selected for the task forces already had perceived abilities and would have been promoted whether they served on those committees or not, it does not deny the fact that their experience in participatory decisions making allowed management to gain familiarity with their work and ability. Further study is needed to identify the reasons for the initial appointment of these employees to the task forces before any firm conclusions can be reached. Nonetheless, advancement is usually contingent upon experience in work assignments and decision making, and the nature of participatory management provides such experience to employees.

It might be possible that in an organization where promotional opportunities are few, participatory management could become the source of great frustration if it does prepare employees for advancement and opportunities rarely occur. However, those employees who were upwardly mobile probably would have left anyway for greener pastures. Opportunity for experience in decision making at the institution would be more likely to keep those employees longer.

Growth is also a strong component of participatory management. Most growth occurs in work through the process of facing problems and assuming reponsibility for difficult tasks. Where traditional management techniques are in use it is likely that employees will be confronted with challenges of this type, but with strong supervisory direction their opportunity for individual trial and error is more limited. A supervisor might readily delegate an assignment to an employee, but countermand or ignore the resultant action, not allowing the employee to observe the consequences.

The McDonald Corporation, known for its fast-food chain, has developed a training technique which demonstrates the difference this has upon the employee. Their method evolved over a period of years in the training of tens of thousands of people. Whenever a new employee or franchisee is trained in food preparation, a three-step process is used. First, the trainer goes through the procedure, explaining each activity along the way. Second, the trainee is asked to tell the trainer what to do, based on his or her understanding of the previous demonstration and instructions. If the trainee makes a mistake in the explanation, or omits one step, the trainer does not halt the demonstration or explain what the trainee forgot. Instead, he continues with the demonstration so that trainee can observe the actual results. The final step is when the trainee actually carries out the demonstration.

Training instructors have told me that nothing is clearer to the employee than when they see the consequences of their mistake. While no one likes to make mistakes, and they can have serious consequences, most supervisors reached their present positions as often because of what they learned from their mistakes as what was achieved through their successes. To be an effective supervisor, one must be willing to allow individuals to grow through practical experience in coping with a problem. When an assignment is delegated, managers are not practicing participatory management if they withhold the right of the individual to carry out the decision or recommendation, even when the worker may be wrong. One can only hope, as greater input occurs, there will be less likelihood for error.

In many situations, the risk of serious error on the organization can be avoided if the assignment is carefully considered by the supervisor before it is delegated. Selection of a typewriter by a secretary, for example, may impair only that secretary's work if the unit proves deficient. Selection of a computer which affects various departments would more properly be delegated to representatives of those departments, and there would be greater likelihood that individual concerns would be better satisfied.

All of these factors—achievement, recognition, the work itself, increased responsibility, advancement and growth—are enhanced under the participatory form of management. Earlier in this book these same factors were cited as job satisfiers, and so it should come as no surprise that employees are attracted to institutions that practice this technique. It provides the manager with optimal number of motivators, useful in coping with difficult and complex tasks—essential tools when the more traditional motivators such as higher pay, fringe benefits, and improved working conditions do not provide the incentive required. Again, participatory management should serve as no substitute for decent, competitive pay and benefits, or adequate working conditions. Those elements have to be present for participatory management to be effective.

Reducing Worker Dissatisfaction

Since we have considered the advantages of democratic management relative to those elements that employees most appreciate about their work, it may be equally useful to examine whether this technique can deal effectively with those things people most dislike about their work.

The first of these is restrictive policies. In authoritarian settings, policies are usually developed by governance and management, and presented to the employee to implement. In a variant to this approach, some organizations employ a consultative technique. The employees are granted an opportunity to consider the policies prior to implementation, and make recommendations which may or may not be accepted by management. The end result is still the same. Employees are likely to have little sympathy or understanding for these policies when they are not involved in their design and implementation.

In true participatory management, the responsibility for developing the policy is delegated to a committee composed of both management and employees with full decision-making powers. Consequently, there is much greater likelihood the policy will reflect the concerns of the employees, and enable them to implement those policies far more effectively. It does not alleviate management's responsibility for communicating, interpreting, and training. The most effective participatory technique in drafting policies will come to naught if the staff is unaware of who was involved in their preparation, if the members of the committee were not representative, and if familiarization with all elements of the policies does not take place. Management must also be prepared to interpret policy for both public and the staff.

Poor supervision is most certainly a strong source of job dissatisfaction, and more democratic techniques should go far to eliminate this. Much will depend upon the attitude that management and governance take in the selection and evaluation process. Participatory management requires greatly different skills, and it should be anticipated that some supervisors, just as some employees, may not adapt to it. After adequate training and preparation on the techniques, supervisors should be evaluated on their development and progress. This will allow governance and management to identify those supervisors who may be unwilling or unprepared to employ participatory techniques fully, and the decision must then be made whether transfer, termination or further training is appropriate. If trustees and administrators refuse to accept that responsibility, there is little likelihood that participatory management will solve this problem any better than more traditional methods.

It has been stated that under true participatory management, employees select their supervisors, and that ultimately, there would be no supervisors. While this will be discussed more thoroughly in later chapters, participatory management does not require worker selection of supervisors. Governance and management are an essential part of participatory management, given the context in which the organization must operate. Furthermore, worker selection of supervisors does not guarantee that poor supervision will be eliminated; incompetence is not a characteristic unique to the supervisory class. Ideally, supervisors are selected because of their experience and training in decision making, and because they have leadership qualities and talents in organization. As a partner with the employees of a unit, the supervisor should contribute significantly to its progress in coping with its responsibilities.

All things being equal, participatory management should be

superior to other management techniques since it allows the poor supervisor to be checked by the staff, provided that management and governance are strongly committed to the technique, and policies exist to protect employees from reprisal by the poor supervisor.

Joint or committee selection of personnel is practiced in some institutions as a participatory method, particularly in academic institutions, and it is believed that this is also a means of avoiding poor supervision. The reverse, however, is quite possible. One large urban public library practicing "team" selection of unit heads and evaluating personnel for promotional opportunities learned that some management personnel used their vote as a veto, creating serious morale problems in their units, which often resulted in the loss of strong candidates who might have potentially threatened their positions. Changes had to be made to ensure that unit supervisors were protected in their preference in filling vacancies.

Poor interpersonal relations is a common cause for transfer or resignation in many institutions. In traditional management techniques this is treated as a personality conflict and transfers may or may not be permitted, dependent upon the needs of the organization. In a more democratic setting, there should be greater flexibility in job assignments and freedom to transfer if the work situation is unsatisfactory. Both of these advantages should result in lower job turnover, but it may also increase the volume of employee transfers.

In those institutions which employ the participatory style, there is a general impression that neither turnover nor transfers have increased. It is believed that this is due to the greater opportunities for achievement, recognition, growth, and the other elements previously mentioned, and that the increased opportunity for employees and management to work together brings about greater understanding and less concentration on internal personality differences.

An example of this occurred in a small college library which adopted the participatory technique. One of the employees continually complained about the cooking odors which wafted into the work room whenever another employee sought to arrange a hot lunch. This animosity was carried into their working relationship, and both employees sought transfers out of the department through their supervisor. Because no vacancy existed at the time, both employees were counseled to postpone the transfer until another opportunity arose.

In the interim, training on the new management technique was introduced, and both employees found themselves on the library's personnel committee. They worked with their supervisor in developing numerous new policies which resolved long-standing grievances between the employees and administration. Eventually, their supervisor informed them that another vacancy was available in a different department of the college, and both were invited to apply. Both declined and stayed with the library, their mutual differences being forgotten, as their interests turned toward assuming a greater role in the management of the institution.

Poor working conditions are another cause for job dissatisfaction, and it was previously stated that participatory management is no substitute. Nonetheless, this technique might well provide greater opportunity for staff to correct that deficiency than other management techniques. Commonly, the reason for poor working conditions would be inadequate funds. Heavy work load, lack of adequate heating, ventilation, or air conditioning, unpleasant older facilities are less often a question of neglect by management, than the simple fact that the institution lacks the financial resources necessary to hire more personnel or undertake expensive renovations. In libraries, safety is less often a concern, but it is possible that employees might be faced with inadequate fire or police protection.

Using participatory techniques, it is easier to call attention to and communicate the nature of the inadequate conditions. Rather than directing their frustration at governance or management, a committee could develop methods to ameliorate the deficiencies. It is also possible, under true participatory management, for the staff to set priorities in capital expenditures and personnel hiring which would permanently correct the problem.

By and large, it becomes tempting for an administrator to distract employees with participatory methods, as a substitute for decent working conditions, or as a way to defer action on promptly remedying those deficiencies. There are certain basic factors which fall to the responsibility of governance and management, and while these can certainly benefit from employee participation, they are the foundation upon which progressive management should build.

Another source of job dissatisfaction is poor salaries, and the comments on poor working conditions apply equally to this question. It has been stated that under true participative management, economic return is guaranteed to the employee. As productivity increases, and costs are reduced, the benefits should be shared with the employees. That is far more difficult in the public sector, but not impossible to accomplish. Traditionally, management and governance have held control over individual wages, and this may or may not be changed under participatory management.

Joint participation in determining pay adjustments for personnel between employee groups and management is not uncommon, and every institution with a union is familiar with its advantages and disadvantages. It would be difficult, if not impossible, for participatory management to take place if the employee has no opportunity to participate on this issue, and any institution considering the adoption of this technique would do well to determine in advance how great a voice they are prepared to grant the employees.

Adjustments in pay scales, cost of living increases, and establishment of equitable pay scales for new and existing positions are legitimate areas for employee participation, as well as consideration of fringe benefits. Individual merit increases and executive compensation may be another matter. In any event, participatory management can allow employees to set priorities which could correct poor salaries, if governance and administration grant them this authority.

Low status and lack of security are sources of job dissatisfaction which can also be dealt with through more democratic management styles. In authoritarian techniques, the fate of the employee is in the hands of the supervisor, hardly something which could provide a sense of security if the employee had poor relations with that individual. And as long as the supervisor retained all decision-making prerogatives, there was little doubt as to the status of the employee. In professional settings, such a libraries, this a common irritant. Friction constantly occurs between librarians and their superivsors regarding individual rights over certain routines and procedures. Librarians, who must continually submit book orders for approval are not going to feel they have the same status as professionals granted authority over their own book budgets.

In a democratic setting the job rights of the individual can be more fairly established. With adequate protection against arbitrary removal or retribution by a supervisor, backed up with the right to appeal to an independent body, the employee should have a much greater sense of security than traditional methods provide. Even with civil service and tenure provisions, librarians are aware that traditional employment policies have been drafted by management and governance, and there is a bias which favors management in any dispute.

It has been hypothesized that participatory management results in greater creativity on the part of the organization. Relatively few tests have been made of that premise, and the literature does not reveal any empirical studies which have been made on this in libraries. There are several factors which would lead to the belief that institutions employing participatory techniques are more innovative. First of all, the decision-making process includes employees and management and, with both partners contributing to any issue, there is greater likelihood for more creative solutions. Second, with more employees involved in the implementation of those solutions, there is greater likelihood of success and wider impact.

On the other hand, creativity and innovation are often the result of individual initiative. Projects which might be undertaken by an individual because of ignorance of the many barriers or problems might never be implemented if they had to flow through a committee composed of employees and management with other priorities, such as improved working conditions and more traditional and conservative concerns. Further, the participatory procedure generally requires more time. This does not have to occur, but there is a greater tendency for more information to be gathered. It would also require more time to familiarize the participants with the innovation and its potential impact.

This chapter opened, nonetheless, with an example of how a problem could be handled through greater input, and there is likelihood that any innovation could be improved and more easily facilitated through a participatory technique. In addition, the process still allows the individual greater flexibility in the workplace than traditional methods.

In summary, the changes brought about in our society have demonstrated the need for better methods and tools to motivate personnel. Traditional forms of management relied on incentives which are taken for granted by the average employee, who seeks achievement, recognition, satisfaction through the work itself, advancement, and personal growth. In each of these, participatory management offers both the manager and the employee greater opportunity for an effective partnership. There is also some indication that democratic techniques facilitate creativity and innovation.

While participatory management cannot substitute for poor pay, proper benefits and working conditions, it can provide some opportunity to the manager and the employee to ameliorate those conditions. The more common causes of job dissatisfaction, such as restrictive policies, poor supervision, poor interpersonal relations, low status, and lack of security are more readily corrected through democratic management techniques. Having reviewed these advantages of participatory management, we turn in the next chapter to methods which should be employed to implement this technique.

Reference

1. *Staff Committee Appointments and Advancement.* Chicago, Public Library, 1980.

V PLANNING FOR PARTICIPATORY MANAGEMENT

Fɪʀsᴛ ᴏꜰ all, the decision to adopt participatory management should not be made unilaterally. If any administrators are so disposed, they should reread the first section of this book, and even consider whether they have the wrong personality for this method. Democratization is a complex change which should involve governance, users, management, the staff, and any other organization or institution, such as local unions, which have a stake in the library.

There are serious and difficult questions which must be considered, such as how broad and deep should participation be granted. As we have seen, there are few instances where complete participatory management has been tried, and those examples are chiefly in business and industry where certain elements such as economic return for employees presented a controlling factor. Many of the partners in this decision will be unfamiliar with the advantages and problems of the technique. Any of the partners could veto the conversion, which would create morale problems among staff whose expectations may have been raised by the prospect. Even if agreement is achieved among all the parties, there are further deterrents to consider, such as organizational changes, legal barriers, financial restrictions. If those are successfully bridged, then there is the necessity of training management and all levels of staff so they are prepared to implement the changes. In short, if you awake some morning with the conviction that your institution should adopt participatory management, roll over and think about it for awhile. It might go away.

Degree of Participation

If you are convinced, however, of its benefits, then the first step should be determining the degree of participation appropriate for your institution. That may change after discussions and work with the different partners, as a result of their fears, concerns, and demands. There are certain convictions which you will have about this method, and it is well to face these as early as possible. The prerogatives of both labor and management are myriad, and it would be well to list these, and determine where you propose each group should sacrifice, compromise, or hold firm.

In democratic management there are no absolutes. The institution that maintains only an employee suggestion box and acts on recommendations is practicing participatory management just as surely as the institution which places all decision making in the hands of its employees. There are degrees of participation and types of workplace democracy. Only management and the other partners in this conversion can determine which is most appropriate for any one organization.

There are several techniques which are not participative, and you should not delude yourself or your staff about them. Consultative management may allow input from employees who will be affected by various changes or policies. As long as management is not bound to accept those recommendations, then participation in decision making does not exist. Open management, or "the open door policy," grants employees the right to meet with supervisors and discuss problems. Again, if the practice does not result in a joint decision arrived at by the affected parties, it is not participation. Use of ad-hoc task forces or advisory committees composed of representatives from the staff and management do provide essential input in formulating policies and implementing change in the organization, but unless those task forces or committees are delegated authority to proceed with their decisions, and as long as management maintains a veto power over their actions, this also is not participatory management. Supervisors who adopt a "participatory style" and delegate responsibility for certain activities to employees, granting them greater flexibility in their work assignments, are not practicing democratic management unless they grant full responsibility for assignments as a right, and not as a privilege which can be rescinded if the work is not performed as the administrator prescribes.

All of these methods have validity, and are commonly applied. All of them are certainly preferable to an authoritarian style with an employee group anxious for greater responsibilities. But participatory management requires management to give up certain prerogatives, the most critical of which is decision making on a unilateral basis. Supervisors must accept the principle that they have an equal vote but not sole power in reaching decisions in the workplace, and that this role is an irrevocable right to the worker. Once that is accepted, the other essential factors to participatory management, with one major exception for libraries, should be relatively easy. Accessibility to management information, communication, protection of employee rights, and the right to appeal a disciplinary action to an independent body are those supplementary elements, while the exception is guaranteed economic return. There are methods of satisfying this requirement, which will be reviewed in a separate section because of their complexity.

Partners in the Arrangement

Once the degree of participation has been determined, the first partner to consider is governance—that is, the library board, institutional trustees, academic authorities, etc. Firmly fixed in American society is the concept of a system of checks and balances, and governance will have genuine concerns regarding the surrender of some of its powers and duties to an employee group. Usually chief executives derive all of their powers through the process of delegation by higher authority. They are rarely in a position to grant powers to employee groups, since such powers are usually not theirs to give. The approval of the governing body is necessary.

The major problem in any presentation on increasing organizational democracy, whether it is to governance or any other partner, is the absence of empirical evidence concerning the benefits of this technique in a public institution, and comparative evidence of its impact on similar institutions. In the case of trustees, there is likely to be particular hesitation in accepting this alternative because the board views itself as the advocate for the user, and evidence of participatory management impact upon that group is entirely absent at this moment.

In a business or industry, the user or consumer has some protection against abuse through the profit margin. Thus, if the employees of a car wash elect to reduce their work schedule, they will suffer reduced economic return when the public ceases to use that facility and visits some other car wash with more convenient hours. The employees of a library, on the other hand, could take similar action and the public would have little recourse but to accept the consequences, and of course, convey their displeasure to the governing authority of the library for failing to represent their interests.

Governance, therefore, would have a much greater concern over actions which an employee group may take regarding policies having impact upon the user. In most institutions that covers a lot of ground, and a large prerogative. While it may help to convince the governance that any delegation of decision making to an employee group would be certain to have management representation and guidance, it should be realized that the board views management as an employee charged with carrying out its policies. Abdication of that responsibility, in part, reduces the effectiveness of management as the spokesperson for governance.

The best method of implementing participatory management in a public service institution is in phases, with preliminary attention devoted to improvements in the workplace and in policies and procedures which have limited if any impact upon the user. The experience of success will help governance to accept this change, and when evidence can be provided that greater democracy actually improves service and employee efficiency, this will contribute to understanding. Almost certainly, if the trustees are convinced of the benefits of participatory management, and agree to delegate decision making on public-service policies, they should participate in the decision making that occurs. That device should also reassure governance that it will continue to have a role as a representative of the user. That also has implications for orientation and training, and it commits the governing authority to preparing itself for this change in practice.

Involving the user in participatory management presents some unique problems whether the organization is public or private. In business or industry, the user is clearly involved through the purchase of goods or services. Buyers, can clearly "vote" by taking their business elsewhere if they are dissatisfied with the turn of events. On the other hand, most firms that practice democracy in management or are employee-owned or governed generally proudly proclaim this fact, for the traditional belief is that the quality of the goods or services will be higher since the employees take greater pride in their production or delivery.

In a tax-supported institution, the public has a clear stake in the changes that take place in the management of the institution, for after all, they own the enterprise. There are several alternatives which can be employed, and there is little experience on which to determine which is the most effective. First, the library could involve representatives from defined user groups to serve on some of the decision-making committees concerned with public service policies. In an academic institution those representatives would probably be elected or selected from the faculty and the student body. In a public library, there could be representatives from Friends organizations, the City Council, the Chamber of Commerce and the like. Presumably, those representatives would have a vote, rather than sitting on an ex-officio basis, since they would soon lose interest without the power to participate in the decision

making. That would further dilute the power of the governance, employees, and management, however, and may
therefore raise some objections among the partners.

Another alternative would be informational, with notices
and releases issued informing the public of what is proposed,
and inviting them to submit their concerns through governance or management. It would be logical to schedule a
hearing on this change and present information on the implications for public service. It might also be logical to schedule
hearings on changes in public service policy achieved through
employee decision making to permit input from that constituency.

There are numerous examples of user participation in decision making in libraries. One public library in the midwest
scheduled a hearing on the results of a policy decision by its
board, based on input from staff, which provided for a reduction in services and the number of branch libraries as a means
of balancing its budget. The Board and staff had established
priorities to bring staff salaries to a competitive level and improve working conditions. Without adequate funds to accomplish this, the decision was reached to reduce public services.

Rather than object to the decision, the public voiced its
support, but requested that a referendum be held to determine
whether additional tax support should be provided to avoid the
reductions in service. Individuals present at the hearing volunteered to form a campaign fund-raising committee to better
inform the general public of the alternatives, if the Library
Board agreed to place the issue on the ballot. This occurred
during a period in that city where every tax increase measure
was consistently defeated.

In response to the community suggestion, the Library Board
did place the issue on the ballot, and true to their word, the
citizens formed a campaign committee which subsequently
raised sufficient funds to publicize the issue. The measure
passed by a two to one margin, guaranteeing that the staff pay
would be adjusted, working conditions would be improved,
and that no reductions in public service would be required.
Both the community group and the Board were so pleased with
the success of the joint effort that a permanent library citizens

committee was established to support the institution and to respond to major changes in public service policy developed by the Library's Board, management, and staff.

At the very least, the Library does need the input of the user when major changes are proposed which may have some impact upon them. If the issues are clearly stated and the need can be supported, there will be far less conflict and more general understanding and support.

The management team will have a critical concern in the application of participatory management techniques to the institution. Some may support the change based on a misunderstanding of what it implies, and great care should be taken to review what is proposed. It would be very unusual if some objection to the change did not arise. Most supervisors gained their position only after long years of service to the institution or to the profession, and they may be very reluctant to sacrifice their rights and privileges as administrators, and to divest themselves of what they believe is well-deserved recognition, for the uncertainties of a new management technique with limited evidence of success.

Here is where further discussion of the extent of the participatory process will be essential, and the understanding reached with governance may require amendment to satisfy fears and concern. Again, it will be important to explain that decision making will not be given up. It will be shared. Many will realize that this is only a logical evolution in the management process, advancing from merely gaining the input of staff on changes affecting their activities, to joining them as equals in deciding upon future changes.

In some institutions where participatory styles have been evident, some middle management personnel consider participation only within the context of greater supervisory freedom. Informed that their supervisor is delegating authority for decision making to them, middle managers may be well satisfied in winning that freedom, but loath to delegate that responsibility either in whole or part to their personnel. Breaking that deadlock places the general manager in a dilemma. He or she is tempted to mandate the further delegation of that responsibility to the unit, but in doing so, the manager would be guilty of the authoritarianism that he or she is trying to end. On the other hand, inaction on the part of the manager will not solve the problem.

In that situation, the manager can either solve the dilemma by reviewing the issue on the basis of an institution-wide policy, or on an individual basis with the middle managers involved. It is possible for an organization to tolerate a variety of management techniques, and most institutions experience this, with supervision covering a full spectrum in a very large library, from authoritarianism to laissez-faire. But participatory management is contagious, and the adoption of the technique by one element of the organization will result in pressures for its adoption throughout the system. Since the method draws upon broad representation from the employees and management on matters which have system-wide impact, it becomes extremely difficult for one unit, such as technical services or reference, to exempt themselves from the process. There may well be some exceptions to this, and every chief executive contemplating conversion to democratization will have to weigh the relative benefits of allowing one unit, either because of the reservations of its supervisor or of its staff, to exclude itself. The benefits of the process should become evident to the unit eventually, and the pressures to participate may become overwhelming, and that might be sufficient reason to avoid mandating a change which really requires commitment and willingness to compromise. It would be reasonable, nonetheless, to ensure that the manager and staff of that unit attend orientation and training sessions on the technique and its conversion, so they understand it, and are prepared for the time when they elect to adopt the method.

Introducing Participatory Management

Introducing this change to the staff will be equally difficult, for there is certain to be suspicion that this is another means for management to exploit the worker. If the staff is represented by a union, that organization is likely to voice some suspicion. Most employees have had some introduction to participation in decision making, too often with the result that the recommendation or opinion of the employee is ignored or only partially accepted. Participatory management is always much easier to implement when the staff itself initiates the concept and petitions for its introduction. Regrettably, that is usually when management is less likely to support the change and becomes suspicious of the staff's intentions.

The first bridge to cross in introduction of the concept to the staff is to define what degree of participation is planned, and how it is proposed to be achieved. Selection, election, or appointment of the employees to the various committees requisite for this technique will be a critical issue. Clearly, if management appoints employees to the committees there is the definite probablity that only those most amenable to management's ideas will participate, and greater democracy will remain only an illusion.

On the other hand, appointment by the union staff association may result in equal misrepresentation. It is rare that any union or staff association is truly representative of the entire body of employees of the institution. Furthermore, union philosophy is that the only rights which an employee has are those which are won at the bargaining table, so there may be more of a tendency for the union to select individuals with greater strengths in negotiating than in knowledge and concern over the issues to be discussed by the various committees.

Selection by the governance of the institution or the users would be difficult because of their lack of knowledge of employee strengths and management structure. That leaves us with the necessity to give a joint committee from management and the employees the responsibility of jointly determining who will serve on the decision-making committees. Discussion on the dynamics of these committees, and their composition and maintenance will be presented later in this book, but it is important that this issue be faced early in the introduction of this conversion to the employees.

The degree of participation is equally certain to be controversial to the employees. No matter how progressive it may have seemed before review by this constituency, management is certain to be viewed as authoritarian and undemocratic when the plan is evaluated by the staff. Since this has been previously reviewed by governance and management, there is a likelihood that severe restrictions may have been placed upon decision making and the rights of the employee. If so, and if there is some distance between the various constituencies, then the only method to arrive at a consensus is through a joint discussion involving representatives of the partners in the plan.

At this point, it might be well simply to acknowledge that some differences exist which will have to be resolved through joint conference, and note that further study of the technique will be required by all parties, as well as training in the procedures. Following that it could be realized that either more or less decision making and employee rights will be required. The differences which exist in each institution prevent any standard formula from being applied.

With the introduction of the plan to the partners, the institution can enter into the study stage. While I have reviewed the introduction of participatory management from the perspective of the chief executive, it should be realized that any one of the partners—the employees, governance, the management team, and even the user—could have initiated the process. While the success of democratization requires the commitment of the chief executive, the same can be said of the other partners. Reluctance on their part will certainly reduce the effectiveness of the technique.

In this major change, the retention of a consultant on participatory management should be considered. Because of the implications to the partners, this alternative merits joint discussion. The relative advantages and disadvantages of consultant agreements are well known, and selection criteria can be found in various texts. The principal factor is that the decision to retain a consultant should be jointly arrived at, and the selection process should also be mutually acceptable to the partners. Nothing would be worse than to reach this decision unilaterally.

Issue to be Considered

There are a host of factors which must be taken into consideration before the organization plows ahead with the implementation of this management technique, and it would be well for management and the employees to gain some experience in working together cooperatively in studying these elements, reaching decisions, and reporting back to governance, management, and the employees.

There is no particular order or priority to each of these issues, but the committees will have to test the plan relative to each issue. If there are unresolved differences, such as the degree of participation in the decision-making process, then both the management and the employee position must be considered.

Certainly one of the issues will be the financial implications of the change, and if there was ever a skill required for this team, it will be cost accounting. Governance will have a concern about the budgetary impact because of its short-range and long-range plans, and the effect upon public service. Management will need to determine where decision making may influence its capital and operating budgets, and whether there are likely to be demands for additional personnel to compensate for committee work and training. There are also increased costs which can be anticipated for improving communications and distribution of management information. Employee concerns will also enter, for there will be a need to determine if the agency will compensate them for travel costs for committee meetings if the facilities are widely dispersed. All of these expenses could affect wages.

Much of the information on this question at the formative stage of the study will have to be of a tentative nature, for it will be difficult to anticipate where differences on various policies will require additional meetings, and whether some expenses will be relatively fixed, or will fluctuate with improved productivity. Nonetheless, the institution must have some approximate range for the expenses of this conversion, or criticism of poor planning would certainly result. Moreover, the cost estimates at this stage will be useful documentation for other institutions planning similar changes, and will serve as a budget control for the employee and management committees.

Another committee will be required to analyze potential or probable changes in organizational structure and staff complements resulting from this conversion. In a smaller organization these are likely to be less evident, but in larger institutions, with more sophisticated bureaucracies, there are some positions which may become redundant. An example might be the position of ombudsman, which was established in some institutions as a means of assuring greater input for the employee. The experience in business and industry is that bureaucracies tend to become simplified under a participatory system, and many inspectional, quality control and foremen positions are eliminated as workers assume greater responsibility over their jobs. However, those were in situations where tangible economic returns went to the employees whenever streamlining could occur.

The committee will be required to plan and hypothesize what the implications of greater democratization will be upon the organizational structure and personnel of the institution. It is mandatory that if any displacements are likely to occur, or additional personnel will be required, that this information be communicated to the committee involved with studying the financial impact of the conversion. Further, alternative placement will have to be considered for those persons likely to be affected by the conversion.

The legal issues will probably require outside counsel, unless the institution is fortunate enough to have someone with the necessary credentials. The basic questions will fall into two areas: 1/ whether the governance can transfer its powers to worker-management groups, and 2/ what guarantees can be provided to the employees to protect them from arbitrary retribution by the supervisors. The question of confidentiality of certain management information will also bear scrutiny from the perspective of the laws and regulations of the state, city, and institution. While personnel records are generally considered sacrosanct, an independent judiciary reviewing disciplinary action taken against an employee by a supervisor may demand access, or the supervisor may present confidential personnel information against an employee.

The legal issues require definition, and governance, management, and the employees should be prepared in this committee to present their questions and obtain the opinion of counsel before they initiate any changes in management. Legislative changes may also be required to remove barriers in some instances, and care must be exercized to ensure that other institutions are not threatened by these revisions.

Because of the relatively limited number of public institutions that have adopted real participatory management procedures, questions are certain to be raised for which there is no precedent. Once these are identified by the committee and counsel, some policies will be required to guide governance, management, and the employees on those questions. One example would be the guarantee of employee rights. While it is true that the Constitution and the Bill of Rights provide some protection to an employee, the courts have generally held that certain rights are the prerogative of local governance and the Constitution or federal regulations cannot override these rights. Some understanding may be required between the governing body and the employee group as to what would happen in the event the governance changes and wishes to reclaim responsibilities delegated to the staff.

Almost every library is imbedded in another bureaucracy, and the interaction with and requirements of that parent will affect the effectiveness of the conversion. A university, school board, or city personnel department may well have regulations governing job assignments and personnel practices that will come in conflict with the library. As one example, a municipal library developed a progressive affirmative action plan through the efforts of a joint management-staff committee (which was granted decision-making authority by management). However, the city's personnel department vetoed it because it was not in conformity with its own management-developed plan.

The limitations imposed by these other layers of bureaucracy may render meaningless some democratization, unless an accommodation is reached. Otherwise, the committee studying this aspect of the conversion may do well to simply strike out certain areas of potential decision making because those areas are the province of the parent institution.

Civil service restrictions and requirements have been mentioned in a previous chapter, but they may provide some barriers to greater democratization. Designed to protect employees from the excesses of management or outside influence, grievance and appeal machinery may conflict with the needs of an organization practicing greater workplace democracy. On the other hand, a careful analysis may reveal that sufficient safeguards already exist to ensure employee rights.

Financial and budgetary procedures are almost certain to be jealously guarded by the parent organization, and prevent the degree of participation desired by both management and employees. Or the process may be rigidly set by law. It will also be necessary to determine whether the financial authorities will approve and support needed expenditures to implement the management changes. Untangling the skein of connections and interactions which must occur between the library and other agencies and institutions will certainly be the obligation of the library's management, and it will be up to it to gain the cooperation and support necessary to proceed. But employees will also need to understand the delicate balance which often exists with these agencies, and recognize why some aspects of the library's administration may have to be exempted from the technique.

Training will require a separate committee of the staff and management, and it will be among the most critical of the committees since confusion about the technique and inadequate training will result in certain failure. The role of each participant in the method must be understood, and the techniques will have to be practiced.

One of the criticisms of the committee structure necessary for this method is that one or two strong individuals could easily come to dominate the groups and skew decision making. Rather than reflecting the consensus of the employees and management, the decisions end as the pronouncements of a strong manager armed with information reflecting the view of the administration, or the union representatives dominate the proceedings with their negotiating abilities. Effective training of the staff, and some practical experience, should prevent that from occurring.

There will also be a tendency to back away from a commitment to the entire staff, and prescribe training for a selected group of individuals, perhaps the professional staff alone, because of the time and expense of training supportive personnel and the belief that they will infrequently be involved in committee participation. To be most effective, the entire staff should be involved in decision making, not an elite group. Exclusion of any category of employees from training provides a convenient excuse for excluding them from any participation in the program.

Improving communications will be another important component of the training. Invariably, any management technique is dependent upon good communications, but the more sophisticated the procedure, the more people need to be informed, and the greater likelihood that essential information will be lost. Each of the committees will be required to report on their decisions and prepare policies and procedures to ensure consistency of action throughout the system. Clarity and conciseness will be requisite, and the training will have to include that element.

Training will require the skills of someone familiar with participatory techniques. It will also require someone able to inform staff on the techniques of group dynamics, and the preparation of reports and systems and procedures, as well as a specialist in explaining efficient communications procedures.

In this chapter we have considered the steps necessary to plan for participatory management. Those steps have included the selection of the initial form of participatory management to be proposed for the institution, a decision of the role each of the partners should take in this conversion and a review of their potential concerns. There has been consideration of the issues which must be studied in advance of the implementation of the plan, including finances, organizational change, legal implications, relations with parent organizations and other institutions which will be affected by the conversion. The importance of training has been stressed.

These have been only a few of the considerations which exist in the conversion of any institution to participatory management. The committee charged with the overview of this conversion study should carefully examine its library to identify other unique considerations. The existence of an employee union or staff organization has been considered in this chapter as synonymous with the employee. However, where there are several organizations representative of different categories of employees, it may well call for a special study to determine how representation on the decision-making committees can be apportioned fairly. There are certain to be other unique elements in any institution, and this process of study should contribute to a better understanding of the interaction of those elements in the operation of the library.

In the next chapter we will give consideration to the implementation of democratization of the organization and the various mechanisms which are required to accomplish that purpose.

VI STRUCTURES FOR PARTICIPATION

THERE ARE several assumptions on which implementation of participation in management rests. The first assumption is that of management, which usually believes that its employees are familiar with existing policies and procedures and the general governance, organizational structure, financing, and goals of the institution, as set forth in official documents. Management believes this because invariably it has been involved in the preparation of those documents. They guide the daily responsibilities of administrators, who are held accountable for them by higher management and ultimately by governance. That assumption is generally wrong, for few of these documents touch the lives of the average employee, except for the policy or procedure with which they may be directly charged to implement.

The second assumption is that of the employee—that management is aware of the practical application of those procedures and policies in the employee's specific unit, but due to the need to satisfy other requirements imposed by higher management or governance, management is either unable or unwilling to grant sufficient resources to allow the employee to adequately discharge his or her responsibility, Again, that assumption is generally wrong. Most managers do not know accurately how their employees carry out their assignments. They assume the assignments are performed as the procedures specify, rather than in some other fashion. Most studies of basic employee training indicate that supervisors delegate this

91

task to someone who has familiarity with the routine in that department, and the individual learns experientially, rather than by the book.

In addition, most supervisors genuinely believe they are not exploiting their staff nor ignoring their needs to satisfy the demands of some other level of management. If they did not make this assumption, there would be a much greater willingness to share responsibilities on the job than is usually evident.

The third assumption is that with participatory management the major work occurs in committee and that everyone has an equal opportunity to contribute to the policy or procedure under review. That is only partially true. The major work in participatory management occurs at the workplace, where the employee is granted greater flexibility to proceed with assignments, which conform to both personal goals as well as those of the organization. While it is true that committees and task forces devote considerable time to joint decisions on the policies and procedures of the organization, if that was the major contribution of participatory management to the workplace, it would have appeal only to those organizations whose principle function was the generation of policies and procedures. Also, we know that the chief function of most committees is not the generation of ideas, but rather the reaction to ideas which are presented to its members, not all of whom contribute to an equal degree.

Need for Orientation

All of this leads to the point that neither managers nor employees are typically aware of what the other does, and the implementation of any democratization inevitably leads to the need for orientation to some fairly basic elements about the institution. Before a committee composed of employees and management devote any time to the revision of personnel policies for the library, for example, they will have to go through an introduction to what the present policies are, learn how they are administered and interpreted by the personnel department, and identify some of the key problems in their use.

Every progressive library and institution provides its employees and management with an orientation when they first join the organization. They usually receive some sets of policies, or have access to them. Somewhere there will be an organization chart, and there may also be a document stating the goals, objectives, and plans for the future. Regrettably, these are only familiar to those who use them regularly, and those who were responsible for drafting them, who are usually the same people in upper management. Now that decision making is being delegated to a level lower in the organization, there will have to be a great deal of orientation to these documents and materials, or the wheel will most certainly be invented over and over again. Of course, in the process of this review, there are also likely to be some changes which will be proposed. That is well and good, for there is still a greater chance of continuity. So, the process of change begins with the past and the present, and while that may seem mundane, it is necessary if all the participants are to be at a level of competency which will allow them to contribute through the mechanisms required for conversion to participatory management.

Familiarizing the managers with the problems of the workplace is yet another challenge. Their ability to understand what employees propose to do in changing their jobs to permit greater efficiency will depend on their familiarity with the procedures workers employ. But an examination of the written procedure, provided one even exists for the task, is likely to bear little resemblance to what and how it is actually done. Libraries are not unique in their inability to design methods to maintain policies and procedures manuals. All of us seem to be far better in writing the original procedure than in keeping it current.

As libraries have increasingly automated, and public service policies have been influenced by these and other philosophical changes, policies and procedures have been left primarily as historical documents, rather than as training and orientational tools, or tools to help with further systems analysis or job description aids. The documentation essential to the operation of the institution is usually only updated when major reorganization occurs, as when a new management system is introduced.

It has been suggested that democratization of the job would lead to an elimination of most policies and procedures, since the typical worker is given greater control and flexibility over his or her assignments. But on the contrary, more democratization will lead inevitably to greater reliance upon documentation about the institution and its operation. We shall see why this is true later in this chapter.

The basis for revamping existing jobs is an updated summary of current procedures. Once that is completed and studied, the management member of any joint decision-making committee or task force, as well as the other members of the committee who are not familiar with the job, will be in better position to understand what changes are proposed, and how they will affect the organization.

Committee Structure

There are two major vehicles for consideration of changes and for implementing policy decisions. These are the committee and the task force. The committee is the most common management device and social institution, outside of the family, that society knows. There are probably more committees than families in existence in the world today.

The composition of the committee can be determined by various sets of factors. There normally are representatives from governance, the users, management, the employees, various unions or staff associations, the parent unit of government, vendors, or other groups concerned with the outcome of the committee's considerations. In participatory management, the basic tenet of committee representation is that all constituencies having a concern in the topic be represented. Further, the group that they represent be responsible for selection. Breakdowns in communications occur when one of the parties affected by the outcome of the discussion and decision misses a decisive meeting.

For example, the selection of a number of new furnishings for the staff lounge would necessitate representatives from the staff and unions, management, the vendor, the parent organization which may have custody over the facilities, and the purchasing department of the library since they will have to implement the orderwork. And then there is the representative from governance, which is certain to have a committee concerned with facilities.

There is no standard size for a committee, although experience shows that the larger the group the more difficult participation becomes. That often has to be compromised in an effort to ensure representatives from among the constituencies affected by the issue.

There are two basic types of committees—ad hoc and standing. There most certainly will be a standing committee with overall administrative responsibility for the application of the participatory techniques to the institution. It would have the chief representatives of the partners: the chief executive of the library, the president of the staff association or union, the president of the governing body, perhaps someone representing the users, and conceivably someone from the parent institution. Rotation would occur as elections resulted in replacement. More than likely this committee might have authority to create other standing committees or special ad-hoc committees to study special problems.

Appointments to other committees may also reside with this steering committee, since the decision as to who should represent the partners when key actions are taken would require high level consideration. On the other hand, the membership of these committees could be at random or achieved through some electoral process. More than likely, however, the steering committee would have this charge, with the obligation to rotate membership in the standing committees to permit the broadest possible involvement in decision making.

In more complex organizations, the logistics of keeping aware of committee composition, goals, and current projects represent a challenge. Care is required to ensure that constituencies be fairly represented, that the same individuals do not appear on too many committees, and that goals do not overlap or conflict with the assignments of other standing or ad-hoc committees.

Each committee requires a charge or goal. A chair and perhaps a vice-chair are in order. The committee chair can be selected by the general steering committee or elected by the committee members. Because of the necessity to keep a balance among the partners, however, the steering committee often identifies the chair for standing committees, while the ad-hoc committees elect their own. The chair has considerable responsibility in this democratic structure. He or she would generally be responsible for arranging the agenda, preparation of any documents in advance of the meeting, maintaining a record of the meeting, subsequently reporting to the constituencies of progress and activities, and drafting any policies and procedures necessary for consideration by the committee members. Depending upon the resources of the institution, supportive assistance may or may not be available to the chair.

Task forces had their origin during the second world war, when complex developments and research projects, as well as mobilization of diverse but important functions, required the establishment of a new management structure capable of acting quickly and utilizing specialized talents from different organizations.[1] Task forces by definition tend to be ad hoc in nature, and do not necessarily represent all the constituencies of an organization. They may in fact draw upon personnel from outside the organization when special skills are needed. They exist only until the assigned task is completed.

The classic example is the employment of a consultant by a library, together with the members of an architectural and engineering firm, joined with certain elements of governance, staff, and management. The goal of this task force might be construction of a new library, and the members of the task force may be called upon to contribute their own particular talents on one aspect of the project, or provide advice on the entire project.

There is nothing to prevent the steering committee involved in overseeing the implementation of participatory management from organizing itself or any of its committees on the task-force model to avoid the establishment and perpetuation of an eleborate bureaucracy, provided that systems and procedures have been created to ensure balance, consistency, and efficiency in the democratization of the institution.

The best advice on committee structure is to keep the number of standing committees to a minimum, and rely more upon ad-hoc groups. This will provide more input and participation in decision making, reduce problems of monitoring the independent actions of committees, and keep the number of groups in control. Use of task forces to arrive at specific conclusions which can then be evaluated for their impact upon the organization by the representatives on the various committees should also streamline their work.

Committees are concerned chiefly with the evaluation of information and assessment of data to determine relative advantage or harm to the constituencies represented on the committee. There may in fact be little interaction between the members of the committee. Committees, by and large, are deliberative bodies rather than generators of new information or ideas. In contrast, task forces are goal oriented. Properly composed, the specialists that are represented on the task force may generate new information required by the other members of the organization to act. They are also committed to the delivery of that information or recommendations on a timely basis to allow their colleagues on the task force to use that data to complete their own assignments.

Drawing upon the building program once again as an example, the committee form would not be as useful as the task force because of these inherent differences. However, in a democratic management style, representation and input is not as readily achieved through a task force. In combination, the two groups will provide the essential balance. Every new building, for example, begins with a written program statement, and that could be effectively prepared by a task force with the members drawn from the affected units of the library, each charged with stating the requirements of their respective units. Meeting together, the task force can identify overlaps and conflicts, and reach a conclusion regarding the final document.

Since groups do not write, individuals do, the task force with its clearly-stated responsibility and group evaluation is the logical means for generating this document. Democratic management methods would then involve the review and acceptance of the building program by the representatives of the constituencies concerned with the project. Once accepted after deliberation by the affected committees, it would go back to the task force to convert the building program into final plans and specifications. The task force would consist of outside specialists and those representatives of the library who were involved in the original drafting of the building program, so they can contribute to the progress of the task force in responding to questions which arise in the conversion of the program statement to actual plans and specifications. The task force would then submit its completed plans and specifications to groups or the joint library committee that approved the original building program, to allow input from the affected constituencies. In this fashion the best use can be made of both the task force and the committee mechanisms, and participation in the project by governance, management, and the employees can be achieved.

Types of Committees

To understand the complexities of committee work and the necessity for organizational discipline and clear direction, it is valuable to arrive at a typology of activities which that structure is likely to involve. Lawrence Bass developed such a typology.[2] He defined six types of committee activities—unoriented unstructured discussion, oriented unstructured collaborations, oriented structured programs without constraints, oriented structured projects with constraints, and last, projects under executive direction.

Unoriented unstructured discussions are those in which the members of the committee have the opportunity to voice their concerns or perspectives regarding the goal of the committee or the topic under consideration. These usually appear at the early stage of any activity, when it is important that the members of the group come to understand opposing viewpoints.

The roles of the participants can become more clearly identified, but this type of committee activity rarely leads to any specific conclusions or action. There is a definite risk that this early discussion could consume most of the energy and time of the participants.

Oriented unstructured collaborations are those activities of committees which are more closely focused on a problem or topic. At this stage some leadership becomes apparent, or at least the expertise of the various representatives becomes recognized in their area of specialization. Participation in consideration of the topic is optional, and the members of the committee decide on whether to contribute based on their interpretation of the discussion from the viewpoint of their specialization. Some decisions may be reached, but principally through persuasion rather than by consensus. At this stage there is likely to be some stimulation and creativity, but the efforts are still not well focused, and individuals may wander off the course in pursuit of their particular interests.

Oriented structured programs without constraints are those activities of committees which have reached the stage where the groups have begun to discipline themselves. They should have developed a general plan of action, and have selected a chairperson to coordinate this effort. The influence of the chairperson is still weak, in that his or her power is limited only to those decisions the committee members are willing to accept and act upon. The chair can draw upon group consensus to move the group somewhat forward toward its goals, but the voluntary and informal nature of the committee at this stage prevents major progress.

Oriented structured projects with constraints are those activities when the committee focuses both on the problem or project and the time constraints, and grants authority to the chairperson to make assignments. At this point consensus is reached on major issues based on competent opinion and requisite participation. Interaction occurs between the representatives relevant to the goal of the committee. Much of the degree of progress is still based on the ability of the chairpersons, and their styles as team leaders. Because of the time constraints there is likely to be less innovation.

Projects under executive direction are those activities of

committees which are directly and sharply focused upon a problem. The chair has been determined previously by management, or in a participatory organization, by management and staff, and the chair possesses delegated authority to assign responsibilities to members of the committee. (Rather than being a stage of committee evolution, this is often a type of committee organization which bypasses the previous stages.) The committee could also simply consist of representatives who immediately assign this authority to the chair. The advantage of this type of committee is that it is able to act decisively, and to proceed with the implementation of the conclusions under the authority and guidance of the chair. Disadvantages are that it may not allow all of the concerns of the constituencies to be expressed and there may be less opportunity for creative interchange among the participants. Solutions may be less innovative. On the other hand, a committee chair who believes in the participatory method could achieve a balance in granting that interchange, drawing out each of the committee members so they may express their concerns and contribute their expertise to the problem.

As seen in this typology, the effectiveness of the committee structure in decision making is considerably influenced by the role taken by the representatives and by the committee chair, and the clarity of the responsibilities given to the group. In its worst stage, participatory management exercised through the committee mechanism could result only in inconclusive discussion. Or, democratic management policies could be defeated by the authoritarian exercise of delegated power by chairpersons. The work of the committee and the role of the participants will be more closely discussed in a forthcoming chapter, but there must be mechanisms in participatory management which monitor the work of committees, and we shall turn now to a discussion of those mechanisms.

Checking on Committees

The most common method which is used in participatory management to evaluate and monitor the work of decision-making committees is the written or oral report. Each committee, ad-hoc or standing, and each task force is given a charge or goal. In the case of ad-hoc committees and task forces, and occasionally, the standing committees, there should also be a time frame for completion of the charge. These units should always be granted authority to modify the charge or time frame in view of special problems they may experience, but when they do so, they should be required to notify the manager or steering committee of their change and the justification. This ensures that someone monitors their work to see they are not becoming unreasonably delayed through endless discussion or poor chairmanship. That may seem like an authoritarian tactic, but it is essential if the weaknesses of one segment of the process are not allowed to affect the participatory efforts of other structures in the organization.

Assuming that a steering committee has been established to monitor the work of those committees granted decision-making powers under a participatory system of management, the steering committee should establish certain guidelines regarding reporting, if that is the monitoring method they elect to use. The reports should be defined as to whether they are oral or written, and whether progress reports are desired. If so, the frequency of those reports should be prescribed. The final report of the committee or task force should be requested by the specified deadline. The steering committee should also determine whether it or the assigned committee or task force will assume the responsibility for dissemination of the reports to management, staff, and governance, and what form the distribution of that information will take.

While this may seem elaborate and a restriction upon the freedom of the committee, it should be realized that any organization must be accountable for its actions. Under an authoritarian form of management, assignments might be delegated to a task force or committee without decision-making power, and the recommendations or report required by the manager could be accepted or ignored, and would not necessarily be made available to affected employees, other levels of management, or governance. As noted in previous chapters, a characteristic and a requirement of participatory management is accessibility of management information; the reporting required of the committees and task forces provides that information as well as allowing some monitoring of progress by all the partners.

An alternative to reporting as a means of monitoring the participatory mechanisms is a liaison technique. Assuming, once again, that a steering committee exists to ensure the effective operation of the participatory system, individual members of that steering committee could attend the meetings of assigned task forces and committees to determine whether problems were being experienced that might demand changes in committee membership, chairmanship, or goals. Reports could then be made to the steering committee by the liaison for action. This technique avoids the expense involved in the committee reporting technique, but it does not ensure access to information on the work and progress of the committees for the various constituencies.

Either or both of these techniques might be appropriate depending upon the nature of the committee assignment or the policies adopted by the participatory steering committee. In some instances the steering committee may wish to audit the methods of the committee chairpersons to ensure that full participation is being obtained from the committee. That cannot be readily determined from either a written or oral report on committee progress prepared by the committee chair, and the members of the committee may not provide the necessary feedback to the steering committee. As another alternative, the steering committee could request evaluations from each committee member to assess their opinions regarding the effectiveness of the committee chair and the committee itself in its progress toward its goals and the extent of participation experienced.

Another tool which serves as a monitoring device, but is more of a communications method, is the written policy or procedure. As noted previously, this is important documentation for the efficient operation of any organization, but especially vital to a participatory form of management. If management delegates decision making to joint management-employee committees, there must be some systematic means of keeping other affected units of the organization aware of those decisions. While reports can provide information on the outcome and consideration of discussions on these changes, these are usually narrative in nature and not written in terms of the interface between different units of an organization. It is possible that the report of a committee could consist of a new or changed policy or procedure, but more likely it would be a statement of the various positions of the committee members, and a conclusion based on the consensus achieved by the committee. The implementation of that change requires preparation of a formal policy or procedure. That is the only way the work of the organization can be documented.

Under more traditional management methods, policy or procedure is drafted by management, or by a committee assigned that responsibility by management. Following review and amendment by the responsible manager, the policy or procedure is either disseminated and implemented by the employees, or presented for approval to governance, and then disseminated and implemented, dependent upon the authority delegated to management by governance. Under democratic techniques, the policy or procedure is either drafted by management and subsequently reviewed and amended by a joint management-staff committe, or drafted at the outset by a joint group. Then it is disseminated to the affected units, unless governance retains its powers of review.

Since committees are better designed to evaluate than actually to write policies and procedures, the most effective methods would be either to have this documentation drafted by management for subsequent review by the committee, or to assign someone (on the committee or a specialist in drafting policies and procedures) to do the drafting. Given the importance of this documentation to the institution, and to the effectiveness of participatory techniques, the more desirable of these alternatives would be to have a specialist in the organization have responsibility for working with the committee in developing the draft. This will ensure that the committee has the utmost input in the development of the document, and still assure consistency with the balance of the organization's policies and procedures.

Full discussion of the form of this documentation, its maintenance and organization requires a separate book, but there are some basic considerations that should be kept in mind. Most organizations are complex enough so that changes in any aspect of its policies and procedures are certain to impact other units, some of which may be overlooked by those who are making the changes. A specialist in policies and procedures can advise a decision-making committee of the potential impact or conflict.

Second, assignment of the responsibility for preparation of a policy or procedure on an arbitrary basis to the members of a decision-making committee is not the most certain method of obtaining a clear and concise document. That responsibility is great enough to effectively preclude individuals from participation in discussion on the issue. Assumption of the responsibility to draft such a policy or procedure by the committee chair also limits the ability of that individual to keep the committee moving toward its goal, and soliciting input from its membership.

The analysis of most tasks to ensure accuracy and reflect the special facets of the work and their interrelationship with other tasks in the organization demands experience and training. It is demanding enough to merit recognition as an essential supportive function which should be drawn upon by the decision-making committees when they have reached the stage where this expertise is required. This specialist can also relieve the committee of the responsibility for disseminating the approved document throughout the system, and ensure the deletion of outdated policies and procedures and the amendment of related statements.

Communicating Committee Decisions

While issuance of revised policies and procedures will serve as a communication device on the end result of the committees' work, and the committee reports will further contribute to the staff's awareness of what is happening in the organization, it does not satisfy all the information needs of the various constituencies. Additional mechanisms are needed to permit greater interaction among the departments and partners. The most common device in libraries, as well as other organizations, is the staff newsletter. Most frequently it is generated by management, and it expresses management's views or interpretations of the actions of governing and administrative authorities. In some instances, input from users and employees may be encouraged, but since editorial power rests in the hands of management there is little likelihood of divergent views or opinions being expressed. A contrast is often found in the publication of the library union or staff association. Where those publications do not exist, or where they are not received by management and the governing board, some correction is necessary. Both management and governance deserve the right to communicate their concerns and views to the employees, and it is unfortunate that the "house organ" is usually viewed in a derogatory fashion. But it is equally vital that staff have a voice, and either funds should be set aside in the organization to permit this, or editorial policy and the composition of the existing newsletter should be altered to grant that participation. An editorial board consisting of representatives of the employees and management might be one means of achieving that goal, provided that staff are protected from reprisals for statements in the newsletter which may be critical of management views.

Some may see this as a means of fomenting confrontation, and point to the personal attacks and statements they consider inaccurate in staff and union newsletters as examples of what may occur if improved means of communication is granted to employees. However, such statements are usually the result of lack of participation, understanding, or information. If staff are involved jointly with management in decision making, then there is less likelihood that criticism of new policies and procedures will occur. There will be minority opinions, but those are to be encouraged, for they need expression and may influence deliberations on issues by the committees. Personal attacks or criticism based on inaccuracies are anathema to everyone, and it is probable that good judgment would prevail in a jointly directed staff/management newsletter that would ensure protection of individuals against this type of invective.

It is always in the best interest of the organization to ensure that effective communication exists among the staff and management. While there are costs and problems in achieving this, there are equal costs to be borne by the library if this issue is ignored. Arriving at a balance necessary to satisfy the needs of both management and the employees, and keep within the budget, is most appropriately a decision which should be shared between the two parties.

An issue which is often raised in communication of employee and management information is privacy, and the pertinency of certain financial or personnel data. Public institutions are naturally influenced by the legislation of their state or parent institution. For example, in most states, the salaries of public employees are a matter of public record. Salary schedules and hourly rates for various job classifications are published. Revenues and expenditures are also available. In some instances, even the private investments and business interest of public employees can be obtained.

Nonetheless, there are still many issues where employee rights and the right of the public or the organization conflict. For example, should the home address and telephone number of any employee by available for examination by another employee or the public? Normally we would say not. But what if there are some residency requirements, or a staff/management committee determines that for emergency purposes this information should be accessible? If the organization is planning to acquire some property for expansion, should the purchase and bidding strategy be made known to the employees and the public? Or will this result in an owner obtaining an unfair advantage, and the cost of the property being increased? Policies on the issue of privacy are of concern to governance, management, employees and the public, and they should be arrived at jointly. Participatory management may create greater problems in areas such as this one, but the technique also offers better means of resolving them.

Staff meetings are another major means of achieving greater

communication. For both large and small organizations, there may be barriers to holding these as frequently as desirable. Large library systems with branches scattered throughout an area may find it impractical to close down these units and bring in the personnel for a program. Smaller libraries may lack sufficient staff to cover public service points, and may find that it is against the policy of governance or the parent organization to close agencies even briefly to allow such a meeting. Scheduling staff meetings after hours on personal time works a hardship upon those who may have other commitments to family or career.

The best method of resolving these problems is on a participatory basis. Communication is a commitment for this method of management which all of the partners should realize. Governance and the users may wish to maintain the full service schedule, but if the organization is to operate efficiently, they will have to recognize that even libraries are like machines. They most go down periodically for maintenance, and staff meetings are definitely maintenance routines. Certainly there is a balance which must be found, and the variations employed by libraries to permit meetings are myriad.

Several essential elements are necessary to an effective staff meeting. There should certainly be a planned agenda. Under participatory techniques, this would be developed jointly between management and employees. The meeting should open on schedule and adjourn on time. Delays or extensions establish a bad precedent and are certain to conflict with individual schedules. If everyone knows the meeting will begin on time, they will be there or lose the benefit of that portion of the meeting. It would also be desirable if attendance at the meetings was mandatory, with allowance for personal conflicts such as vacations, etc. If attendance at staff meetings is purely voluntary, then the benefit of good communication is lost, and the employee or manager who misses the session is less able to assume responsibilities under a participatory scheme.

Staff development also offers an important means of communication. Any institution entering into more democratic management methods has an obligation to allocate part of its budget to allow for this training. In business and industry, one to two percent of the personnel budget is commonly applied for this purpose. Among libraries that portion is likely in practice to average less than one half of one percent. Libraries are supposed to be concerned with education and personal development, but we set a poor example.

The reason for greater commitment to staff development under participatory management techniques is because of the greater flexibility of job assignments that individual employees are likely to experience. As they grow in responsibility, there will also be greater necessity to prepare them for that role. The organization is more likely to involve itself in various innovations, and it will require expertise in those fields. Maintaining the ability of the staff to cope with these new challenges and responsibilities requires a training or staff development officer, or if funds are not available for this purpose, at least the formal assignment of these responsibilities to someone on the staff. That individual can ensure that opportunities for advancement are not lost, and that key personnel are developed for greater responsibilities in the future.

In conclusion, we have considered various mechanisms useful or necessary for the implementation of participatory management. Improved orientation, the use of ad-hoc and standing committees or task forces, various communications techniques such as reporting and committee liaison and evaluation, the use of policies and procedures, the role of staff newsletters and general meetings, and the importance of staff development. None of these mechanisms are novel but each will contribute significantly to the application of democratic management in the workplace.

References

1. Bass, Lawrence W. *Management by Task Forces: A Manual on the Operation of Interdisciplinary Teams*. Mt. Airy, Md., Lomond Books, 1975.

2. *Ibid*. p. 15.

VII ROLES IN PARTICIPATORY MANAGEMENT

IN PREVIOUS chapters we have devoted attention to the planning required for participatory management, and to some of the mechanisms and methods which are required for its successful application. Some attention should be given to the role of each of the participants—the chief executive, the management team, the employees, governance, and the user. There is a complex relationship which must evolve. Understanding of the interaction required helps to identify potential friction or problem points and the adjustments that can be made to ensure a smoother operation.

Chief Executive

The chief executive officer of the institution is the key element in participatory management. Opposition from this source to its use, or misuse of the technique by management can raise the greatest barrier to its success. The chief executive has a unique relationship with governance and the parent organization, which hold the manager responsible for the operation of the institution. The chief administrator selects and directs the management team, and sets the tone or style which influences their own role in the organization. The user most frequently works with the staff, it is true, but if there is a serious problem, the buck stops with the chief executive. Consequently, the user is likely to be strongly influenced by the attitude and policy of the general administrator regarding the management technique used in the organization. Staff realize that the chief executive is most frequently the chief negotiator and, in any participatory system, will be responsible for final consideration of a policy or procedure.

It is possible for an organization to convert to a democratic technique or method of management without the support of the general administrator, but it is dubious whether it would be either effective or last very long. The chief executive will also have the most difficult role to play in this change. Management must pull together all the varied strengths, weaknesses, fears, and expectations represented in the structure. If force is applied to any of the partners in this change, the setting is ruined. If the management team is reluctant to participate in the change, it is always possible and tempting to decree that all members must join in the effort. Even if consensus is thereby achieved, there will be those who will not participate. As the method gains hold, there will be pressure upon the executive to force their inclusion.

Staff will always be reluctant and suspicious of any measure which grants them greater responsibility without assurances of improved economic return. While there are many motivators that exist which can offset these feelings, chief executives should realize that they are adversaries in the minds of many employees, who will be quick to note exceptions in the democratization of the organization. For this reason, the decision to proceed with participatory management will have to be taken with caution, for it will be difficult to arrange a reversal and maintain a semblance of commitment. The chief executive cannot be participatory one day, and then withhold support of a decision which may appear unwise on the following day. It is like pregnancy—either you are or you are not.

The chief executives who have experienced problems with their use of participatory techniques most frequently are those who have not carefully planned for its introduction, and not fully prepared the management team and employees in the use of the techniques. They may have introduced it only to discover that personnel have arrived at decisions which were deficient due to inadequate information. Or they may discover that the decision-making committees were dominated by authoritarian-style employees or managers. Or the systems necessary for the communication of new policies and procedures were inadequate and the organization is still employing the procedures developed under the former management style. Those portions of the organization that have not elected to participate may be clashing with the more democratically managed units of the organization. For this reason, the role of the chief executive should be to test the readiness of the many facets of the organization to accept and succeed in this new technique before each step is taken. That caution should be exhibited not as reluctance, but out of concern that the conversion is successful.

Organizations do not change overnight. There are learned patterns which have to be altered. There are commitments to certain goals, and large investments in equipment and procedures. The role of the chief executive must be to assure those with commitments to existing methods and goals that they will have the opportunity to participate in any consideration affecting them, and the manager will have to keep that commitment.

Trust will also have to be evident in the attitude of the chief executive. Most management systems are designed on the assumption that the individual worker cannot be trusted. The hierarchial organizational structure is built on the assumption that everyone's actions must be reviewed by someone else higher in the pyramid. While participatory management does not dispense with accountability, it does grant the individual or the participant groups the authority to reach a decision and act without being subject to review and reversal by a higher authority. If a chief executive does not have trust in the ability of the management team and the employees to reach a responsible decision on an issue, then the executive should not delegate that decision.

That should not serve as an indictment of chief executives or cast doubt on their commitment to participatory management. They are paid to use their judgment in making assignments, and if the personnel who would normally be expected to participate in making decisions do not have the ability or knowledge to properly act, in the judgment of the chief executives, then they would be naïve and foolish to delegate that authority. Instead, the executive has the obligation to see that individuals receive the training to qualify them for responsibility, or see that they are removed and more competent personnel hired to allow the organization to adopt greater democracy in management.

Once the decision is made to delegate responsibility in some area, however, the executive has the obligation to give full support and commitment to ensure success. Several years ago a small midwestern public library gained a grant to experiment with an innovative means of extending service to the disadvantaged. The director of the institution hired a project director and delegated to her full responsibility for hiring personnel, setting policies on a cooperative basis with her staff, and taking any actions necessary to ensure the success of the project. Although the project had certain goals and a tight budget, the project staff was granted authority to make essential modifications in the goals, and transfers within the budget, if they could justify the changes to a small advisory committee consisting of the director, governance, a representative from the library staff, and several outside representatives of the funding organization and the community.

The director intended to test not only the innovative technique in extension, but also whether greater democracy in the administration of the project would prove transferable to the library itself. One of the first decisions of the project staff was to shift to a more flexible work week. Rather than the 40-hour work week with regularly determined starting and stopping times the project staff set their own schedules, and their work week expanded or contracted based on the needs of their clientele. The average remained forty hours, but the project staff were entrusted to keep their own time record.

When a member of the project staff quit, the staff decided to assume her responsibilities and divide the salary among themselves. After some discussion, the project staff later voted to terminate all fringe benefits for themselves and convert this to direct cash. The book budget for the project was also allocated among the members of the project team, and several of the members of the team elected to purchase materials through local book stores to ensure more rapid acquisition for the clientele.

At each point, the library director supported the decision of the project director, and where approval was required from the project advisory committee, he took the side of the project team. After two years, and some significant changes in the budget and goals, it was evident that the project was successful in significantly increasing library usage among the disadvantaged people of that community. Surveys conducted of the clients by independent sources revealed that the users were excited about the service and wanted to see it continued as a permanent part of the library's program. Despite this success, both the governance of the institution and the staff opposed its continuance and the service was ended upon the conclusion of the funding period.

In subsequent analysis it was determined that the real reason for the failure to maintain the project was not lack of sufficient local funds, as was announced, but resistance of both governance and staff to the participatory elements introduced in the project by its director and the project staff. First of all, the library staff was aware that salaries were significantly higher, even though job titles remained the same. While it was recognized that the project staff had willingly assumed greater responsibilities and workloads, and gave up fringe benefits voluntarily, the library staff resented what it felt was favoritism to a special group.

The flexibility granted in work hours also irritated the regular library staff, and so significant a barrier arose between the two groups that they even established different lunch hours so they would not have to intermingle. Regular library staff also resented the conversation of the project personnel, which tended to focus on their techniques in working with their clients, while the regular staff tended to focus on family and personal issues. Conflicts arose between the Library's technical processing personnel and the project staff over their use of local bookstores as sources for their materials. The technical services department took it as a personal insult that they were bypassed, and expressed concern about bibliographic control and fiscal accounting.

This example demonstrates that the role of the chief executive in supporting participatory management is often not sufficient. Management also has the obligation to ensure that there is support and understanding between all the partners in the organization or there will be friction and resistance.

Rensis Likert theorized that each organization has personnel who function as link pins between various groups.[1] These individuals must have the authority and respect of the group in which they are normally a part or member, as well as the group in which they may serve as an advisor or liaison. Link pins exist at many different levels in any organization and they serve an important role in sharing information between the groups, gaining consensus in those groups, and representing the interests of their own group as a delegate to other structures within the organization. More than any other individual in the organization, the chief executive must function as a link pin, healing the rifts which are certain to occur, conveying information and the viewpoint of the varying groups, negotiating and compromising to ensure that confrontation does not occur, and helping all the constituencies to achieve their goals.

The responsible manager under a democratic system is not one who lets "everyone do his or her own thing." If there is a potential source of friction between the various units or constituencies, the manager must bring this out, and see that it is resolved. Had the library director in the previous case study informed the project team of the growing friction with the regular staff, and identified the major points of conflict, and then worked for resolution between the two groups, there is a likelihood that project would have become a permanent part of that library. Instead, he viewed his role differently, and the project failed.

Management Team

The role of middle managers is equally difficult. Caught between the intention of the chief executive to delegate decision making, which was formerly their responsibility, and the staff's demand for a greater voice in management, there may be a tendency for some middle managers to abdicate all responsibilities and shift the full burden onto the staff. Some may be protective of the rights of some personnel under their direction, or anxious about the ability of staff to cope with problems which they have been unable to solve even with years of experience and training. There may also be a feeling of betrayal, based on the assumption that the chief executive lacked confidence in their ability and was turning to the staff in an effort to bypass them. Certainly many middle managers will have positive feelings toward the technique, and recognize that it will provide motivation and opportunity for their personnel, as well as advancement and growth for themselves. Nonetheless, some middle managers will be ambivalent in their feelings, and the chief executive will have to provide reassurance and preparation if that is to be counteracted.

The lessons learned by management will be conveyed in practice and in instruction to the employees. The principle role of management in preparing for the conversion is clearly as teacher. Even though formal instruction should be planned, there is necessity for practical experience to reinforce the instruction. Delegation of responsibility can begin in stages which should provide confidence to both the supervisor and the employee, and begin to build the level of interaction to the point that participatory management does not become set on the calendar as pre- and post-conversion.

The middle manager must also serve as guide, introducing the employee to the various tools necessary for participation in decision making. Familiarization with management reports and recognition of their significance, introduction to the policies and procedures of the system, and review of the plans and goals of the organization should not come all at once, but should be introduced as relevant to the operation of the unit. Departmental meetings should begin to be planned cooperatively.

The manager also has to prepare for the implementation of this new technique. While formal preparation and instruction should occur, many of the methods can best be learned experientially. There is need to identify not only as a representative of management, but also as a voice for the unit in the decision-making process. The middle manager is another link pin. Is the manager's position based on the consensus of the unit, or based on his or her opinion as the manager of that unit? In some situations one or the other will have ascendancy. But the manager should be forthright in saying which it is.

Managers have a major role as communicators, for most of the information in any organization flows to them. In more traditional management techniques that information did not have to be shared, but now it must be, and that will lead managers to serve more and more as interpreters to their employees. Because of the emphasis on participation, the employees may react or recommend changes which must be communicated back to the decision-making body, or the chief executive.

As changes are proposed in policy and practice, the manager will increasingly serve as an initiator of action requests to decision-making bodies, and expeditor in their satisfaction. The recommendation of staff to replace equipment in the unit may no longer require justification to a chief executive, but to a committee having responsibility for allocation of funds for capital purposes. Whoever makes the decision, the supervisor is still the initiator of the orders, and approves the condition of the equipment when it is received.

The manager still reports on the progress and work of the unit, and continues to function as a member of the administrative cabinet for the organization. There is no great metamorphosis which takes place in the traditional role of the manager, but only in the way in which decisions are made and work is performed.

Staff Members

That is not true of employees. Accustomed to carrying out the duties assigned by managers, the work and role of the employee was generally as prescribed in the job description, together with "other duties as assigned." Under a democratic management there is a shift to a more generalized statement of responsibilities, together with "other duties as assumed."

Perhaps the greatest danger in conversion to participatory methods is that the employee's expectations are raised too high. They may assume that they will participate in all decisions, and that is unlikely and impractical in larger organizations.

Under organizational democracy, the employee becomes a partner or co-equal member of the team that will decide on issues which are delegated down to the unit. Typically, that involves decisions on the employee's individual work methods and assignments. Given the need for a technical processing unit to prepare books for public use and for bindery, it may be possible for hours of work, individual assignments, processing methods and other elements of the work to be determined by the constituents of that unit and management. In addition, it may be possible for the decision on book selection policies or personnel benefits to be delegated to a joint management and staff committee, on which the technical processing unit may be represented. Decisions as to who will represent the unit on those committees could be delegated to the unit. Thus, participatory management may be more narrowly defined as representational management depending upon the need and role of the employee. It does not mean that the operation of the unit or the institution is turned over to the employees.

Employees also assume a new role as innovators. Under more traditional management methods, changes in procedures or services were imposed by governance or management. However, democratic techniques allow, and in many cases require, that the employee initiate reforms in jobs and services as well as working conditions. It is of little value to the worker or the organization if steps are taken to allow greater voice in the direction of the organization, and nothing is proposed. While management certainly has a responsibility to initiate and facilitate innovation, if the employee is to become a true and contributing partner in the decision making central to the institution, there should be commitment to improvement is service as well as in working conditions.

Traditionally, the worker has always served and been recognized as a specialist. Assignments were made based on the skills the worker exhibited. In a democratic system, employees must carry their roles as specialists one step further, and serve as representative and consultant in that specialty through the decision-making process. The decision to automate circulation in a library may find a clerical employee speaking not just as a representative from the staff, but also as a specialist in records management and public relations. It is important that this transition take place, or each decision-making effort will degenerate into a labor-management question, rather than a group of specialists contributing their expertise to the solution of a problem. Just as the manager must at times represent management, and at other times the unit, employees must recognize the duality of their positions and roles.

In that capacity, employees serve a related role, and that is as reactors. Participation demands more than mere attendance at meetings to consider issues, but the free and unrestrained expression of the employee opinion. Employees are entitled to their opinion on issues, but it is important that it be identified as such, and separated from that of the individual as specialist or representative of staff or unit. The employee who is not prepared to contribute in decision making should have the wisdom to decline the responsibility, and permit another the opportunity.

Another role of importance to the employee is as communicator. Service on a policy-making committee is a two way process of communication. The employee has the obligation to react on behalf of colleagues, and also to carry back to them the results of the committee's work. In many instances where representation is granted to staff, administrators are amazed when staff reaction to a decision in which they had representation is negative. The administrator believes that the employee will relate progress on the problem and convey to the committee why and when compromises are necessary. The error is in failing to explain to employee representatives what their role is in the process. Not only are they on the committee to state the position of their colleagues, but they are expected to keep their colleagues informed and convey their reactions back to the committee.

While communications and reporting methods should be established under any participatory scheme, redundancy is often useful. There is rarely a situation where too much information is provided to staff and management. Further, personal interpretation is more rapid and provides flexibility in getting to the specific concerns of a special constituency.

Not much has yet been said about the role of the employee union or staff association. They may have a large role in some institutions and entirely represent the employees in the process of building participatory mechanisms. It is believed, however, that where that occurs it would be possible to substitute those organizations for the role or position identified for the employees. The major concern that the chief executive and management should have is whether those organizations truly represent all of the employees. It would be most unusual if they did. More frequently, the existence of a union or staff association demands parallel representation on decision-making committees. For example, a joint committee concerned with revision of employee benefits might have a representative from the union representing tradesmen and custodians, another from the union representing clerical employees, one from the professional association representing librarians, along with a representative from that portion of the staff not associated with any union or association. The larger the organization, the larger the committee and the greater the difficulty in gaining consensus, but there may be no choice, unless the employee associations and unions can agree to some representational arrangement among themselves, which would be unlikely.

The role of the labor union or staff association is certainly as a link pin. They serve to bridge the gap between many units of the organization, and affect both management and employees. They can achieve consensus and considerably improve the effectiveness of participatory techniques. It is also possible for the union to subvert the technique and use each meeting as a bargaining session for employees. The union must recognize that the management technique is designed to allow the employee to enter into the decision-making process as a partner equal with management, and not as an antagonist. If that accommodation can be reached, the conversion to more democratic procedures can advance.

Management should realize, however, that the union does

not intend to give up its position as representative of the employees. If management uses participatory techniques as a means of undermining the union's role or bypassing them, there is certain to be conflict. A good example of this may be the establishment of a joint management and employee committee on pay and benefits. Should the union not be represented on this committee, there will be limited acceptance among the strong union members of any agreements reached. The union is also placed in a dilemma, however, if it is represented on the committee, for it will find itself as an equal partner with representatives from other employee constituencies. Agreements with the employee groups which result in similar benefits may lead members of the union to doubt the relative advantages of their membership and dues.

More likely, the question of employee benefits may have to be dealt with separately by management and organized labor, rather than through a common process with all employee groups. Labor is on record in favor of participatory management, and there is more likely to be support for the steps being taken by management which will allow employees greater freedom in their work and participation in decision making. [2]

Unions can also contribute to participatory management by drawing upon specialists in various fields who can aid task forces and committees to reach conclusions faster. One library benefitted from the information supplied by the union on work standards in various clerical areas. The information was unbiased and allowed the joint management-employee team to arrive at staffing requirements for a new unit which was proposed for the institution.

As noted previously, unions and staff associations have newsletters which perform invaluable service in communicating changes and general matters of concern to the employees. They allow employees to express their opinions and concerns, as well as criticism, on present or proposed policies. Having the representatives of the union involved in decision making will significantly improve the accuracy of reporting on policies and practices to the employees, and allow the library to benefit from already existing communication channels.

The Governing Authority

Governance should not use participatory management as an opportunity to assume management responsibilities of the institution. While there has been reference in this book to the participation of governance in decision making on various issues and as a mediator on some issues, the fundamental role of the governing board is to consider the broad policies of the institution, select its chief executive and monitor his or her performance, ensure that plans and services appropriate to the community are developed, and look after adequate financing of the organization. Meddling in administration is a certain means to undermine the effectiveness of the administrator.

Governance always has difficulty in defining the difference between policy and administration, and while it is hoped that the line is clearly drawn at the time the chief executive is retained, more often than not the distinction between the role of the governing organization and the executive requires continuous review. Both the trustees and the chief executive have a continuing obligation to inform and educate each other, and through that process the benefits of participatory management should become known, just as the constraints to be placed on the process should become established.

Because governance will be asked to allow the chief executive to delegate certain duties and responsibilities to joint management-staff committees, there will be understandable caution on the part of the board. The legal problems which might be confronted in this process have already been discussed, as have the attitudinal questions.

It has been stated on many occasions that the trustee groups of most libraries are rarely representative of their users. There are few academic or school libraries with young people participating in governance, and the board members of most public libraries are more often drawn from the elite of the community rather than the middle class who are the predominate users. Be that as it may, the governing bodies of most libraries consider themselves as representatives of the community, and weigh the recommendations of the chief executive in that light. For purposes of their role in participatory management, that is workable. Someone should weigh the changes which may be proposed in public service by joint staff and management committees from the viewpoint of their impact upon the user. Because of the difficulty of gaining the actual input and representation of the user, the existence of governance on the committee considering such a change is a reasonable surrogate. Again, care should be taken by the governing body to ensure that it maintains its role as a reviewer of policy changes and not as administrator. Should there be doubts about whether governance can maintain that role, then it might be best to follow the traditional method in submission of policy changes to governance and spare them the inconvenience of representation on myriad committees where considerable time might be devoted to other issues than policy. In this fashion, decision making can be jointly shared between staff and management, and then either jointly or unilaterally presented to trustees. Either way, the presentation to governance will be strengthened by the knowledge that both management and the employees have reached consensus on the question, lessening the chance of internal strife when the policy is implemented.

The legal authority should exercise its role as cost benefit analyst on changes introduced through participatory management, since in the spirit of compromise the dollar is often quiet in decisions reached between employees and management. Since the profit margin is not a controlling factor in public institutions, governance will have to exercise controls. That is a traditional role, and the circumstances are no different, with the exception that the pressures upon management will become more severe in a democratic setting.

At times there may be issues on which there is true division between the employees and management, and governing bodies must assume the role of moderator or arbitrator. That has been less frequently a role of the board, since traditionally chief executives had that responsibility. Under a democratic technique, their intercession may not be appropriate, and since it is likely that the division between management and employees will be on matters of policy or finance, trustees would have to face the issue. Again, the difference is that it would be facing positions between the employees and management, and governance is the most likely arbitrator.

Finally, governance should function to support the decision to convert to greater democratization of the institution, and communicate the benefits of this change to the parent institution and the public. Knowing that the intent of this change is to improve productivity and service to the user, provide greater motivation to the library staff, and enhance the opportunity for growth, achievement, and advancement, governing authorities should take pride in the ability of the agency to take this progressive step.

User Participation

The role of the user is difficult to prescribe because of the different mechanisms established among libraries to grant representation and input in the design of services and collections. Some libraries have tried elaborate marketing surveys to assess needs of both users and nonusers. Others rely on suggestion boxes or the comments heard at the public-service desk. Undoubtedly, to survey the public regarding the provision of greater participation in the management of the institution would be unfair, for the public would need to know what the implications to public service are, and that would be difficult to determine at the outset.

Despite the role of governance as surrogate for the user, there will be occasions when public or user opinion should be sought on the impact of a policy change. Certainly the scheduling of hearings or meetings on minor policy changes would be inappropriate, but on critical questions involving clear choices, the user should be provided with an opportunity to react to the change. As previously reported, it may be possible that users have an alternative that governance, management, and staff failed to consider, or discounted. The decision to seek additional tax funds will place the library in the public arena, and the earlier that input is received, the better.

The user should also be given the opportunity to provide ideas on new services, or improvements in existing services.

Here is where marketing surveys do provide a convenient mechanism. Friends groups are also suitable sounding boards for change, and will serve as a staunch supporter for the institution if they are invited to participate in decisions regarding public service: They are often asked for little else but money. The key to participatory management is not to open the decision making process to just the employee, but to involve those constituencies which have a pertinent interest on specific issues. As noted before, participation is contagious, and as the organization gains confidence in its use, there will be even greater involvement.

In this chapter we have considered the various roles and responsibilities of the chief executive, management, the staff, unions and the staff association, governance, and the user. While certainly those points which have been raised are only illustrative, and other duties or roles may be assumed by those partners in the participatory process, it can be seen that these constituencies have complex responsibilities and their interaction will be critical to the introduction of democratic management to any institution.

References

1. Likert, Rensis. *New Patterns of Management.* New York, McGraw-Hill, 1961.

2. Walker, Kenneth F. *Workers' Participation in Management.* Paper Delivered at Second World Congress of International Industrial Relations Associations, Geneva, September 1–4, 1970.

VIII CASE STUDIES

To UNDERSTAND how the methods of participatory management are applied, and examine the roles of the participants, several examples of the techniques in libraries will be reviewed. The names of the institutions are omitted to ensure confidentiality, but the circumstances are accurate and should demonstrate both the advantages and problems presented in using this technique.

A College Library

When the Friends organization of a small college library offered to allocate funds derived from a used-book sale to that institution, the director delegated to his staff the responsibility for determing how the money should be spent. Having some experience with the technique from previous projects, the director asked the president of the union which represented approximately half of the library staff to appoint two persons from among the membership to serve on a committee to determine where the funds should be directed. Meeting with the heads of his public services and technical services departments, he selected four unit heads to serve on the committee, naming the most senior as the chair. With the advice of this cabinet, he also invited two other employees who were representative of the nonunionized staff to serve on this committee.

Since the Friends had not placed any restrictions on the gift, which totalled $2,500, the director told the committee, in a written charge, that they should be innovative and apply the funds to anything within the Library that could improve service or working conditions. Because of the likelihood that this might only be a one-time gift, they should be cautious in allocating the funds towards some service which might be of a continuing nature, such as a subscription to a number of journals. He also asked that they complete their report with a recommendation within 30 days to allow a timely response to the Friends, who were anxious to publicize how the gift would be applied.

The Friends were interested in the method the library director employed, and asked if the chair of the book sale could serve on the committee, on an ex-officio basis, so she could better explain to the Board of the Friends how the recommendation was reached. Since the Friends had an obvious stake in the project, the director had no objection and informed the committee chair of the addition. The chair then proceeded to arrange the first meeting of the committee in the college library seminar room, with expectations of arriving at a decision during that meeting and completing the charge promptly. At that first session, however, the representatives of the union strongly protested the inclusion of the representative from the Friends on the committee, complaining that if the library director really wanted to delegate responsibility for determining how the donation would be used, he should not have tilted the balance of the committee in favor of management.

The representative from the Friends denied she was there to influence the committee, and denied that she was a representative of management's interests. She also noted her ex-officio capacity on the committee. The union representatives indicated that since she could speak on the issues, she would be in a position to sway the participants. They also protested the decision of the library director to appoint the chair, and argued that in a truly democratic management he would have allowed the committee to elect its own chair. In frustration and surprise, and committee chair adjourned the meeting after an hour, and promptly reported the events to the Library director. She suggested that he attend the next meeting and mediate, so that the committee could turn its attention to its charge.

He did this, noting that the reason he allowed the Friends to send a representative to the committee was to ensure they could better understand the justifications for the use of the grant. He defended his appointment of the chair because of the lack of a staff representative who could speak for all the employees. The chair, he explained, was selected because of her experience in handling committee work and her seniority on the staff. The union representatives replied that they appreciated the director's position, but they still felt the committee should select its own chair, or the chair should be selected by the director and the union president. It was noted that while the union did not include all employees, it was the largest staff organization and its officer was elected. Further, they felt the committee should establish rules, and that the first rule should be that ex-officio members not be allowed to speak to any of the issues, since that might influence the outcome of the discussion.

The director called the arguments of the union members divisive, and ruled that the representative of the Friends could speak to any issue. Further, he informed the union representatives that to select a committee chair on a cooperative basis with the union president on the grounds that he represented all the employees would disenfranchise those members of the staff who did not belong to the union. At this point the union representatives informed the director and the committee that since this was not a truly participatory activity, it was pointless to waste their time under the delusion they would fairly contribute to the decision. They left, and the remainder of the committee finally elected to establish an employee recommendation plan using the grant, after brief discussion on other alternatives suggested by the participants.

The union subsequently urged its members not to participate in the suggestion program, stating that it would be rigged in favor of granting sums to only those whose suggestions were favored by management or the library director. They cited the experience of the projects committee as an illustration of the type of democracy practiced by the library director. While the suggestion program was implemented and awards were given using the Friends grant, the director concluded that it was not fully successful because of lack of support by the union.

In this case study it can be seen that while the director had the best intentions, and thought he had set the stage for the participants, lack of preparation turned the experience into a disaster. An understanding had not been reached with the union president regarding the composition of the committee. The participants were not familiar with the technique. The question of the role of the representative of the Friends should have been shared with the committee. The chair was unable to deal effectively with the controversy, and the actions of the director only compounded the problem. Rather than seeking resolution of the differences among the committee members, the director simply moved forward without the union representatives, ensuring their lack of participation in a project which clearly required their support.

A Public Library

At a municipal public library, the city's personnel department sought to strengthen the position and role of that institution's middle management staff and to employ participatory management through the establishement of new disciplinary policies. The library director had recently angered some members of the staff through the establishment of stiff penalties for absenteeism, and they had protested this decision to the city personnel department. That agency interpreted this as an example of authoritarianism that would accelerate membership in the union which was then in process of organizing the library's personnel. In actuality, the library director had enacted stiffer penalties at the request of middle management staff who demanded a more stringent policy to correct what they felt was an abuse of sick-leave arrangements.

Discussions between the city personnel director and the library director resulted in a decision to establish a committee composed of staff, with some management representation, to evaluate all the present library disciplinary policies and remodel them on a participatory basis. The city personnel director suggested that all major job classifications and units be included in the committee, but that the director do the appointing. Care was to be taken that the union or other staff associations not be officially recognized, but that members of those organizations be included. A solid manager competent in committee work was to be appointed by the library director, and a clear charge and deadline was to be given to the committee.

The library director proceeded with this, but explained to the committee that while it was granted flexibility in revamping the policies and its recommendations would be strongly supported by him, it would be necessary to seek the final approval of the Library Board, since it was the responsibility of that body to approve all library personnel policies. Given that caveat, the committee proceeded. Anxious to determine how the work of the committee was progressing, the city personnel director called the library director and asked if he could send two of his staff over to observe how the discussions were proceeding. It was noted that the staff members had extensive knowledge in the development of personnel policies and could function as a resource to the committee. After it was agreed that the specialists would only observe and contribute upon request by the committee members, permission was granted by the library director. He subsequently notified the committee chair, and told her to explain the role of the observers, and the restrictions. The director told the chair of his hope that the committee's decisions were truly participatory, and that every effort should be made to gain involvement and consensus. The committee consisted of 15 persons, and each was to be asked to contribute to the deliberations and to share the results of those discussions with their colleagues. Further, the purpose of the committee and the names of its members was publicized through the staff newsletter and a special memorandum. Suggestions and concerns were invited from the staff, to be directed to any member of the committee.

At the next meeting of the discipline policies committee, the observers from the city personnel department grew concerned that too much discussion was taking place and interjected suggestions on key policies based on their experience in working with other city departments. After discussion with their supervisor the following day, the city personnel director called the library director and informed him that he felt the committee chair was not effective, and allowed too much discussion among the committee. He also expressed concern that the policies would favor the staff rather than strengthening the position of the supervisors, and recommended that the library director add some additional management personnel to provide better balance.

The library director explained his instructions to the committee chair and felt that since many of the committee members were unfamiliar with committee work and participatory techniques, some time would be required before they could function more effectively. The early sessions of the committee were, in fact, required to train the personnel and give them confidence in participatory techniques, the library director stated. He also gave his support to the committee chair. As an alternative, the city personnel director suggested that the middle managers be given an opportunity to contribute to the policies following completion. The library director indicated his objections, explaining that this would ruin the motivation of the committee, if they realized their decisions would be modified by management. As an alternative, it was suggested that a preliminary draft of the policies be sent to all supervisors to be reviewed with the employees in the units, with objections and other feedback to be directed to the committee for preparation of a final draft. This was agreed upon, and subsequently discussed with the disciplinary policies committee, which also supported broader participation by the staff.

Several months passed and the work of the committee progressed more rapidly as they gained familiarity with committee work and participatory techniques under the guidance of the committee chair. The observers from the city personnel department periodically attended the meetings and attempted to influence the discussion, but because of the pace, they became frustrated and finally ceased attending at all, expressing their disappointment to their supervisor regarding the nature of the policies. When the committee was ready with its preliminary draft, the library director notified the city personnel director of his intention to distribute the draft to the unit heads for review with their employees, as previously agreed. He also indicated his intention to circulate the draft to the union and various staff organizations at the library to obtain reaction.

The city personnel director registered his strong objections to the latter strategy, explaining that it would set a bad precedent if those employee organizations would be asked to participate in the decision making, since that could be considered as official recognition of a right which had not been granted through collective bargaining. He further explained that it was against city policy to officially recognize unions or employee organizations and exercised his authority by directing the library director not to forward copies to those organizations or to solicit their opinion officially. The library director acceded to this order, with the realization that the union and staff organizations would most certainly obtain copies of the document and would be certain to react through their representatives who held seats on the discipline policies committee. Although he could not gain the official position and involvement of those bodies, it could be obtained indirectly.

Copies were distributed to all units with instructions to supervisors that the draft was to be circulated to all employees, and their suggestions be solicited and sent back to the committee. The suggestions were to be kept confidential from the supervisor if the employee so wished, and members of the library director's management team were requested to monitor the process so that greater participation could be assured. Members of the discipline policies committee were also made available to units that requested them to explain why they arrived at certain recommendations, and to hear various concerns expressed.

After a reasonable period elapsed, and the deadline passed for submission of suggestions, the discipline policies committee reconvened and after deliberation made necessary changes in the policies to satisfy the concerns of the staff and supervisors. The final draft was submitted to the Library Board by the director, and with his endorsement, the measure was adopted without change. Subsequent to this, the city personnel director contacted the library director and expressed concern about certain aspects of the policies which he indicated might have adverse legal implications and directed that the policies not be implemented until his staff and the city legal department reviewed them.

The library director noted that if the city personnel department had concerns about the outcome of the decision-making process and wished to retain veto power over the staff committee, that it should have stated this at the beginning. He argued that it would undermine the morale of the staff and management if their decision on these policies were to be reversed or amended. The city personnel director indicated he would exercise his authority to protect the interests of the city and prevent the library from using the new policies. The library director indicated that the library board also had certain powers over its employees, including the establishment of personnel policies, and the city personnel director was overstepping his authority. Rather than enter into a jurisdictional battle, the library director suggested that the city personnel department examine the legal questions which might exist and return with them for discussion with the discipline policies committee. Action would be postponed pending that review and discussion. This was done, and it was subsequently determined there were few legal problems, and these required minor amendment which was readily accepted by the committee. The city personnel department had more substantial procedural and philosophical differences on the policies, but concluded that the library board had authority to establish policies in the defined areas. The policies were then implemented and gained uniform acceptance and satisfaction among the staff and management.

In this case study there were a number of forces at work, and a number of errors in procedure. The director should have developed a participatory role for the city personnel department, which had an obvious stake in the outcome. Further, the lack of preparation and training for the staff in participatory techniques subsequently delayed the progress of the committee. Nonetheless, the director properly supported the work of the committee, and ensured that their decision-making power, within the parameters which were defined, remained inviolate. The subsequent success of the policies, which had previously been a source of considerable staff unrest, revealed the effectiveness of the technique.

A *Technical Library*

In a large technical library, the director concluded that the institution needed to convert to a COM (computer output microform) catalog in order to reduce costs and improve bibliographic control. To accomplish this, he appointed a task force consisting of members of his management staff coupled with a small number of representatives from among the employees of the institution. They were delegated authority to make the decision as to how the change should be implemented, and opportunity to hire any outside expertise necessary to help them in the process. A time frame for reaching the decision and completing the project was established by the director, but his assistant director, who was appointed chair, was informed that this could be amended if circumstances required.

The chair met with the committee and informed them that the first step in this decision was to visit other libraries that had adopted COM catalogs and see how they managed the conversion. The visits were arranged, and the committee members had the opportunity to familiarize themselves with many of the problems and techniques. Several of the committee members expressed concern that the nature of bibliographic control at their technical library was substantially different than that employed at the usual library that converted to COM. It was their opinion that these differences should be reviewed with the director in view of the problems that might arise if their institution attempted to use the standard methods of conversion they observed. The committee chair rejected that suggestion, citing that their charge was not to determine whether their institution was to convert to COM, but to determine how to proceed with the conversion.

The committee also expressed concern over their unfamiliarity with automation. It was observed that while all had extensive library experience and training, none of them had ever been involved in this type of automation and some consultative help from specialists in the field would be desirable. Again, this was rejected by the committee chair, who felt that while it was within the power of the committee to retain consultant assistance, to do so would acknowledge weakness to the library director. The chair felt that between their readings on the subject, observation of other library experiences, and their own initiative and skills, they could develop the correct approach. Besides, it was noted that their library was unique, and no consultant would have any experience with their type of bibliographic control.

Accordingly, the committee turned its attention to the preparation of a plan and a set of specifications to implement the conversion. This was subsequently reviewed with the library director, who reaffirmed his support for their decisions, and he authorized them to contract with a qualified vendor. Regrettably, the specifications had so many deficiencies and complexities that only one vendor submitted a bid, and he included a number of exceptions. This was reviewed with the library director, and he announced his support of the committee on its decision, to contract with the one source, and charged them with supervision of the implementation process.

At this point, several members of the committee urged the committee chair to reject the bid and reconsider the entire project based on the exceptions which the vendor expressed, and their own doubts about the ability of the vendor to complete the project on a timely basis. Feeling that he had the support of his director, the committee chair rejected that advice. The contract was awarded, and the vendor met with the committee to discuss the implementation process. It was determined that because of the exceptions made in the contract, that the method proposed by the committee could not be utilized. The vendor proposed an alternative based upon his experiences in other institutions. Members of the committee representing the staff objected to the alternative proposed because it would shift a substantial burden of additional work onto the employees. Members of the committee from the Technical Services units expressed opposition because of the inappropriateness of the technique in view of their own unique bibliographic control processes.

The vendor indicated he could not proceed with the contract in any other fashion, and suggested an amendment in costs if another method would be employed. The committee chair rejected that option, and suggested that the vendor compromise on a method that would satisfy the basic concerns of the staff and Technical Services units, be within the capabilities of the vendor, and if sufficient funds did not exist to complete the project, the contract amount could then be amended. On that basis the vendor and the committee then reached a compromise agreement. Representatives of the employees still objected, however, to the method because of the additional workload it would place upon them.

After a period of one year had passed, and the project was still delayed, the library director became alarmed and requested a status report from the committee chair. Although this had been discussed on several occasions, the response had been that the vendor was proceeding according to plan, and the library would soon have its COM catalog. On this occasion, however, the director had received some feedback from members of the committee that serious technical problems were delaying implementation of the project. In the meantime, equipment had been ordered and was received. All that was absent was the COM catalog itself.

Confronted at last with the fact that something had gone wrong with the project, the library director met with the committee and relieved its members of their responsibilities. An individual with experience in the implementation of COM catalogs was hired and given responsibility to continue with the project. This was finally completed, at a cost three times over the original estimate and three years late.

In this case there was no question of the commitment held by the library director to participatory management. That very commitment and unwillingness to interfere, as well as the lack of monitoring or reporting, was part of the reason for failure. It was also evident that the management style of the chair conflicted with the participatory technique. Rather than permitting the genuine participation needed to ensure the success of the project, the method allowed an authoritarian the freedom and power he needed to dominate the project and ignore all recommendations. The employee representatives were alienated at every turn, and the likelihood of their support was minimal.

As evident in this example, use of the participatory technique can lead to serious problems when the wrong personalities are involved, when employees and management are not prepared for its application, and when effective monitoring and communication are weak or absent. The library director simply dropped the assignment into the hands of a group of staff members, and divested himself of all responsibility. That may be delegation of decision making, but it is also poor management.

A State Library

In a state located in the southeast, the state library sought to establish a pattern for multitype interlibrary cooperation, and elected to use a participatory technique to achieve that end. The director of the state library contacted leaders among the various constituencies and asked for their suggestions as to who should be asked to serve on a committee to design a plan appropriate for their state, and to draft legislation. Although the state librarian had personnel on the staff and in state government who could have been utilized to accomplish this end, she felt that the involvement of the constituencies affected by this change would permit development of a better plan and much more effective implementation. It was also hoped that the involvement in the decision-making process would motivate the participants to work more actively toward passage of the legislation.

Based on recommendations received from her survey, the State Librarian advised her Board to name 15 persons representative of school, academic, special, and public libraries, as well as representatives from the state board of education, its academic council, trustees, and the major library associations.

The committee was appointed and when it convened the State Librarian reviewed its charge. The committee was granted a budget, and authority to use it for whatever purposes it deemed advisable, whether that involved retention of consultants or travel. It could elect its own officers, and draw upon any resources available in the state through the State Library.

Although some of the committee members had worked together on other projects before, the majority had not, and after some time was lost in discussion, the State Librarian, who served as an ex-officio member of the committee, suggested that the committee might benefit from some consultant assistance. This was agreed upon, and an individual with experience in group dynamics was retained to assist the committee in getting organized and establishing clear goals and a practical timetable. They went into a retreat for two days, focusing not on the problem, but the technique.

The committee then proceeded with its deliberations and identified where information was required, and whether responsibility for obtaining it could be assigned to the members of the committee, the State Librarian and her staff, or special consultants. Individual members of the committee volunteered for several assignments in areas of their expertise, and target dates were agreed upon for the completion of these reports so that they would mesh with the work of other members of the committee. Through the skill of the elected chairperson, each of the participants was eventually involved. Interest was strong, and one of the committee members even changed the date of her daughter's wedding to avoid missing one of the meetings.

The draft of a plan was written based on the cumulative work of individual members of the committee, the consultant reports, and the contributions of the State Library staff. This was forwarded to the State Library Board, with the suggestion that it be circulated throughout the state among concerned individuals and groups to get their reaction. This was agreed upon by the State Library Board, and following a wide distribution and regional hearings, the results were tabulated by the State Library staff for the committee, and amendments were made to satisfy concerns expressed and problems identified.

Legislation was subsequently drafted based on the plan, and with the full endorsement and grass-roots support it had among the constituent groups, it was subsequently introduced and passed by the State Legislature.

Communication throughout this entire eighteen-month process had been from several sources. The State Library regularly reported on the progress of the committee, as did the library associations. The committee members also had decided during their organizational sessions that they would report the gist of the committee's deliberations to their constituencies and keep the committee informed of any danger signals. Once the various library associations endorsed the measure, libraries were asked to explain the bill and plan to their users and legislators.

We do not often think of participatory management techniques in work at this level, but the method is capable of migration both in an institution and externally. In this instance the chief executive, the State Librarian, delegated decision making, with the approval of her board, to a committee representative of the various constituencies who would be responsible for implementing the decision. While they were not employees, and this was not a management/labor situation, the potential for conflict given the different needs and viewpoints was clearly evident. The State Librarian provided her strong commitment to the technique, and gave necessary advice when it was needed. She properly monitored the progress of the committee, and saw to it that progress reports and communication were maintained between the committee and its constituencies. Because of the motivation that came from the application of this technique, sufficient impetus and understanding existed to see that the measure was approved. It is also important to observe the value of adequate preparation for the committee. Had this not occurred, valuable time would have been wasted as the committee struggled for mastery of the essential participatory techniques.

As demonstrated in these case studies, participatory management can be an instrument for success or failure, depending upon when and how it is employed. Given the right preparation and personalities, and the appropriate problems and support, the institution can benefit and the productivity of the participants be vastly improved. The judgment and the knowledge of the participants in this process makes the difference.

IX ECONOMIC RETURN

IN AN earlier chapter, it was noted that the guarantee of economic return to the employee was an element essential to participatory management. Since that presents serious problems to a public institution such as a library, the issue merits special attention. Even though a library is not a profit-making organization, it can be managed as one, and there can be incentives provided to employees.

Every library manager is aware of the necessity to control costs, and knows that individual employee productivity is vital to the operation of the institution. Those concerns are common to any manager, whether they are employed in a profit or nonprofit situation. In the public sector it is generally recognized that taxes, which are the revenues required to support services and institutions, are not rising as rapidly as costs. The only solution is to reduce costs wherever possible and increase employee productivity. In the private sector, managers are faced with a similar predicament. While their revenues are not dependent upon taxes, they are faced with the necessity to sell their service or product. If costs are increasing in the public sector, they are doing the same in the private sector. While private business or industry can raise prices to compensate, it does so only at the risk of reducing sales. Therefore, the manager in the private sector seeks to increase productivity. The principal means of doing this is through motivational techniques such as increasing economic return and participatory management. The library manager has to employ the same techniques to be effective.

Merit Pay Increases

This is done regularly. Most managers have indicated to an employee at one time or another that if work improves, they will seek a salary increase. The problem is that managers may not have the authority to grant that salary increase. They may have to go to a board or higher level in management to gain approval. Or the regulations governing employee pay may be so restrictive that the manager does not have any flexibility.

The obvious solution is to grant the individual manager greater authority to make decisions on salary increases. In governmental settings, given the plethora of regulations that exist, that may be easier said then done. Nonetheless, the principle is essential for any institution to consider in adopting participatory management. The individual manager must be granted as much latitude as possible to reward increased productivity. That does not extend to the extreme where serious inequities are created between the pay levels of different employees performing the same work. It does not bind management to pay the same wage, however, if performance varies between employees.

The most common compromise which exists in institutions today is the merit increase. That is a commonly misused phrase. Pay scales have provision for periodic increments, which may be granted on a semi-annual or annual basis for adequate performance during the preceding period. The institution may misname them merit increases; they are actually longevity increases. While there is nothing wrong with them, for they ensure that incoming employees are not paid at the same level as those who have gained experience with the institution over a period of years, the longevity increase does not recognize merit or increased productivity.

Another adjustment which is periodically granted is the cost-of-living increase. That only compensates the employee for higher expenses or the decreased value of the dollar. To consider a cost-of-living adjustment as an incentive to an employee, or that it recognizes increased value to the organization, is an insult. The only incentive it provides is to encourage the employee to look elsewhere if the organization fails to provide a decent pay adjustment to compensate for rising costs of living.

To provide the manager with the tools required in participatory management, the typical pay plan should include a salary range, with increments for longevity and merit, together with periodic revision of the plan to compensate for the cost of living. While the organization should have policies to ensure that the merit aspect of the plan is not abused, it is fundamental that the manager be granted authority to award merit increments. Further, it should be a clear policy that as the employee improves in skills, or redesigns work in such fashion that productivity increases, merit increases will be granted without long delay and numerous bureaucratic barriers.

The mechanics of such a plan require consideration by management and the employees to ensure that it is fair and equitable. It obviously requires participation by governance, since they must provide the funds for the plan. The merit increase should also be meaningful. A five-dollar pay adjustment is unlikely to provide much incentive to a clerical employee to upgrade typing skills sufficient to increase output by 20 per cent.

Participatory management techniques should also make it possible for an entire unit to obtain merit increases if through common effort they are able to increase productivity. In this fashion, the resentment which might be created when one employee receives an adjustment can be avoided, but the manager should be careful to avoid a situation which provides this increase merely to buy off resentment by individual members of the unit who did not participate in the changes and who will not be involved in them. The same tendency may exist when a manager grants merit increases in such a fashion that it is obvious they are distributed among all the employees as a supplement to pay, or to compensate for what the manager feels is too low a salary for the position.

In many institutions which employ merit increases, there may be a reluctance on the part of managers to grant increases to deserving employees because of fear that they will have to grant similar adjustments across the board. Sometimes a particularly productive employee is passed over in favor of a less deserving individual simply because the latter has not received an increment for some time, while the more productive employee received a merit increase recently. Establishment of some standards, adequate preparation for managers in the use of this tool, and some periodic audit of the practices of these managers should prevent abuse or misuse. Establishment of administrative barriers, such as myriad approvals, will not solve the problem, but will hinder the ability of the supervisor to act.

Attrition of Staff

Attrition is one means for reducing operating costs, and sooner or later every library employs this practice as the least painful means of responding to budgetary crises. It can be the source of valid management and employee complaints regarding increased workload, impaired working conditions, and decline in service standards. It can provide management, however, with another economic incentive for employees.

One southern library experiencing a freeze in its income for the coming year arranged a general meeting of its staff, management, and governance to discuss alternative methods of dealing with the problem. Because of budgetary problems in preceding years, there was little flexibility left in the various accounts. Choices boiled down to a freeze on salaries, or a freeze on job hiring. Management determined that normal attrition would produce sufficient funds to produce a cost of living increase and a small adjustment in salaries, but the existing staff, of course, would have to assume the additional workload created by these vacancies. The alternative of reducing services through the elimination of existing positions was rejected by all the parties.

After some discussion, the staff agreed that they could reorganize their work and assume greater responsibility if vacancies were not filled during the forthcoming year. It was agreed that since attrition might be irregular, some transfers might be necessary to avoid termination of existing services, and management and the employees agreed to arrive at procedures and policies satisfactory to all. In more traditional situations, the governing board and management would have determined all of this, resulting in substantial criticism from employees regarding the increased workload. The use of the participatory technique avoided that problem, and provided management with an opportunity to allow employees a direct economic return for increased responsibility.

This establishes another principle, and that is to allow the manager of any unit flexibility in determining the exact number of employees required for the unit, as well as the level of skills needed for each of the positions. Again, that is not very common in the public sector, for position descriptions tend to be established and fixed, together with employee complements, for budget purposes. It puts the manager and the employees of that unit in a collective straitjacket.

If attrition occurs in a department, the manager and the staff, in a participatory setting, should be able to assess whether the vacancy should be filled, or whether the workload can be redistributed and job descriptions and pay levels adjusted accordingly. All too frequently, even if the employees and management are successful in redistributing the work, they are penalized by losing the position and are given no additional compensation for their initiative.

With some cooperation between budgeting authorities, civil service boards, governance, and the staff and management of an institution, there should be some means of achieving unit personnel flexibility. If some adjustment and reclassification can be allowed, there should still be sufficient savings derived by the institution to satisfy the budget authority. Morale can be improved, productivity increased, and costs lowered. The initiative for this effort is with the chief executive of the library, and if he or she exercises this responsibility and employs a participatory technique in arriving at the necessary decisions, the typical problems created by attrition can be avoided.

Personal Incentives

Cost reduction is a continuous goal of management, but there is usually little incentive for employees to participate in efforts to control costs. At one library a unique set of circumstances occurred which illustrated what can happen when some incentive is provided. This was a college library at a relatively small institution which was faced with the need to reduce personnel. The library director elected to eliminate some of the part-time student positions in the belief that would have the least impact. After the news was broken and the individual students were notified, one of the students visited the director and asked whether he could be retained if he could find some method of reducing costs equal to his salary. On the spur of the moment, and because he was impressed with the initiative the student exhibited, the director agreed, even though he was not quite certain how that could be accomplished with his central administration.

The following day the student returned, armed with facts and figures obtained from the college finance office and the technical services department. It appears that the student had been involved with some extensive weeding that was underway in the library, and he had been impressed by the volume of books discarded. Those books were hauled away by a contract scavenger service and dumped. In short order the student could demonstrate that if the college established a periodic book sale or arranged a sales shelf for students, faculty, and the public, that it could eliminate the scavenger contract and bring in more than sufficient revenue to offset any handling costs. The savings exceeded the young student's salary, and the library director kept his word.

Most cost savings implemented by employees may not be as clear-cut, but the example does establish another principle, and that is to allow the manager greater flexibility in the budgeting of expenses for divisions within the library. Under traditional management techniques the budget process is almost inflexible. If the manager or employees find ways to avoid some costs, the benefits are not returned to the unit. Management may receive some credit, but the money is returned to the general budget.

Management should be provided with sufficient flexibility at the unit-head level so that substantial savings in costs can be returned to the employees of that unit in the form of merit increases. If the cost savings are minor, the unit head should have the flexibility in budgeting to reallocate the savings to satisfy some other need in the unit. A reduction in the cost of supplies in a technical processing department, for example, undertaken through some participatory effort on the part of the employees and the supervisor of that unit, should result in benefits. The savings may allow transfer of the funds to equipment accounts, say, to allow new fans to be purchased.

In most instances this type of incentive to reduce costs involves only an accounting transfer. If governance and management can accept this policy and communicate to the employees what the relationship will be between cost reduction and return, the result will be an organization which is much more cost conscious.

Employee Suggestion Programs

Another alternative is the employee suggestion program. There is hardly anything innovative about this technique and it has fallen into disuse mainly because of the limited incentives it offers to either employees or management. Governmental and educational institutions rarely believe in making significant awards to employees for cost-reduction ideas, apparently in the misplaced belief that every public employee has an obligation to implement cost savings as a normal job requirement. Private industry knows better, and this writer once paid for a year of college with proceeds from one suggestion adopted by the firm that employed him.

There are certainly some drawbacks to employee suggestion programs, and a few barriers. The governance or parent institution may not allow financial incentives for employees. In those instance it may be possible for the library to offer other fringe benefits, such as additional vacation, free parking, a new desk, or similar alternatives. A simpler procedure is to draw funds from other sources, such as a grant from the Friends organization or a local industry or from the Library's endowment.

Another drawback is the investment that must be made in investigating the suggestion. That can be costly and time consuming, siphoning off more personnel effort than the return. There is also the impact this may have on participatory management at the unit level. An employee may observe methods in the unit which can be simplified but withhold discussion of them with supervisors and coworkers in an effort to get a substantial reward through the suggestion program.

Both of these problems can be avoided through policies adopted by a joint management and employee committee. In the first instance, policies can be developed which do not compel investigation of suggestions which a panel deems to be of limited value. A policy can also be adopted which prevents employees from bypassing their own departments in suggesting cost saving measures. If this is coupled with a policy of returning the benefits of cost savings to the unit, that should also eliminate the temptation to collaborate with employees in other departments to bypass the restriction and share the reward.

There are numerous sources of information on suggestion programs. The major program elements should consist of sufficient reward to stimulate interest in participation, joint employee and management planning and review panels, together with a scheme which evaluates the suggestion fairly to arrive at an equitable reward.

Contractual Services

While the Library is a nonprofit institution, there is no reason why it cannot offer its services or the services of its employees on a contractual basis to allow some increased level of economic return for increased responsibilities. For several years there was a small public library in the midwest that contracted with the National Aeronautics and Space Administration to serve as its regional film library. That institution happened to have experienced personnel in the administration of film collections, and a perennial budget problem.

After discussion between governance, management, and the employees it was decided that the library would submit a proposal to NASA to assume responsibilities on a contractual basis. The proposed budget included sufficient funds to allow the library to hire additional personnel and equipment needed for the responsibility, and also to grant pay adjustments for personnel currently on the library staff for the additional work load they would assume under the program. The proposal was accepted, and the library became a government contractor. This happened right at the time NASA was in the middle of the lunar explorations, and films on that program were very popular. The contract granted a sum to the library for each film loaned or shipped to other organizations, and before long 25 per cent of the library's budget was coming from NASA. The employees and managers benefitted from the pay adjustments, and the organization benefitted from the tangible revenues derived from the contract.

While this is an unusual example of entrepreneural initiative, there are opportunities which continually arise for employees and management to creatively improve service and their own economic return. Technical processing is one common avenue. Many larger libraries are often capable of assuming cataloging and processing services for other institutions, but there is often little incentive to do so. A contract might be proposed but would face the opposition of employees and management in the technical services department, who will raise the specter of increased backlogs and already overburdened workloads. If the contract could be translated into increased pay and better working conditions through revenues derived from the contract, management and the employees of the technical services department might find a way of avoiding backlogs, handling the workload, and incidently, improving technical processing for both institutions, through participatory techniques.

This establishes another principle, and that is to allow the manager of a unit and his or her employees the flexibility to adjust salaries upon assumption of additional external responsibilities where these responsibilities lie within the goals and objectives of the institution. The control that governance and management have over this is through their responsibilities for goal setting. That should prevent individual employees or the reference department, for example, from establishing a referral service which might compete with the library, charging individual clients fees for services which should normally be available from the library without cost.

On the other hand, the Library might determine that while it cannot satisfy certain types of questions because of present budgetary limitations, one of its goals would be to establish a reference and research service for clients on a fee basis. The reference department might then effectively work toward a plan on a democratic basis with management and governance which would ensure that no conflict of interest occurs, that existing services to the public are improved or maintained, and that individual employees derive some personal economic return for assuming additional responsibilities on a contractual basis.

Policy Considerations

Any time that productivity increases and cost savings occur, the public benefits and the fact that libraries are not profit-making institutions should not prevent its employees from increasing their earnings in return for their increased workload or broadened responsibilities. Certainly, precautions are necessary to ensure that services and resources paid for by the taxpayer are not withheld. All the partners involved with democratic management techniques have a fundamental obligation to guard the public interest. Too often, however, the employee is exploited in the public interest through lower salaries, increased workloads, and poor working conditions.

It would be poor management to ignore the lessons that have been learned by private business and industry. Application of participatory management methods can lead to greater productivity, lower costs, and increased employee motivation. An essential element of the participatory technique is guaranteed economic return to the employee, and there are methods which public-sector institutions can employ to accomplish that end. They are worth considering by any institution that wishes to make a commitment to greater democratization.

Public-sector institutions do have another means of achieving economic return, and that is through the implementation of greater taxes. Not all libraries have this power, and where it exists at all, it usually requires approval by a parent organization or the direct approval of the voters. Central in the minds of most administrators and governance is the belief that good service will lead to good support by the taxpayer. While that is a tenet of the library profession, there is far from solid evidence that is true. It is more likely that poor support will result in poor service to the taxpayer, which leaves most institutions in a chicken-versus-egg situation.

Generally those institutions which have the most direct access to the taxpayer, i.e., where they must go directly to the voter for approval for any increase in budget, are the institutions which have the greatest incentive to provide good service, a fact which should be realized by governance and those organizations that strive for consolidation of government into ever-larger units. It is extremely difficult for a school or academic library, or a municipal public library, which are imbedded in the body of larger parent institutions, to take their case directly to the taxpayer to seek increases in return for improved productivity. Their programs and needs are subsumed within the budget of usually vastly greater organizations, and until reform in public administration occurs, there are limited incentives for individual units such as libraries to cut costs. If surpluses exist near the end of the year, tradition calls for those funds to be encumbered for fear they will be lost. Public policy has been to treat such waste by imposition of across-the-board reductions, penalizing both the productive and the nonproductive agencies.

The role of governance, management, and employees should be to communicate, to as great an extent as possible, the steps which are being taken to ensure good use of the tax dollar. Involving the public in decision making will significantly contribute to that understanding and provide greater awareness of the need for economic return for employees commensurate with their contributions to the institution. Earlier in this book reference was made to the experience of one public library involving the community in a decision regarding reduction of services. In that example, the community supported the decision to upgrade employee salaries—normally not a popular position—when the alternative was reduction of services. The support granted in that situation occurred because governance, management, and the employees communicated the problem and need, and allowed the public to participate in the decision. The public voted to grant the salary adjustment and maintain services through the imposition of additional taxes.

The principle is that before making a decision to reduce services in order to provide for some necessary expenditure, the user or the public should be informed and allowed to determine whether additional taxes should be provided or the services reduced. Any other alternative will result in a disservice to the public and/or the institution. That should be sufficient incentive to management and employees to work toward finding a means to reach the community, even when there are administrative and political barriers. While raising taxes is never a popular cause, reduction of services, or gradual deterioration of services, collections, and facilities are even less popular. There has been a steady corrosion of service in this century because of the inability of libraries to reach the public directly with their case. Governance or parent organizations have been unwilling to seek adequate taxes. Instead they have taken the easier course of starving the institutions and at the same time failing to grant them flexibility for decision making.

In this chapter we have reviewed the problem of providing for guaranteed economic return for employees, one of the requirements for effective participatory management. Among the devices which have been considered to correct this deficiency in the public sector have been modification of pay plans to provide for merit increases, providing greater flexibility at the unit level to allow personnel changes achieved through attrition to be absorbed by existing personnel, provision for units to benefit from cost savings achieved by the employees and management of those units, employee suggestion programs, and the opportunity provided through entrepreneurial initiative. Some discussion on the use of tax increases as economic incentives was presented, with emphasis upon the importance of public participation in decision making on service reductions and the necessity for openness and good communication.

X PROBLEMS IN PARTICIPATORY MANAGEMENT

ALTHOUGH MANY of the more common problems faced in the application of participatory management have already been reviewed, there are some additional pitfalls which need discussion, together with more thorough review on points only touched upon elsewhere. Methods of avoiding or coping with these problems will be covered in proper context under this heading to allow more comprehensive understanding.

Irresponsible Decisions

The greatest fear that management has when it delegates decision making to employees is that they will create a Frankenstein's monster. It is the usual response by employees that management has been creating Frankensteins for years, and if some errors occur it is only just retribution. In practical application, however, it can be seen that joint decision making still allows supervisors to contribute opinions based on prior experience. No group seeks out irresponsible decisions, and the advice on how that can be avoided will often be sufficient to steer the group toward safer waters.

It is possible that a supervisor may be so hated by employees that they may reject all advice from this source and take an opposing course, but that is a setting which is inappropriate for participatory management. Good supervisors have always

155

sought input from their employees, and now that the employees and the supervisor are arriving at decisions cooperatively there is a greater likelihood the employees will respect the opinion ventured by the supervisor, who is certain to continue in a leadership role with the unit.

Sound decisions require adequate information, participants prepared to understand it and with the capability to act upon it, sound working and organizational ability, and clear alternatives. If management furnishes all of these raw materials, there should be no cause for alarm. But let us assume that management cannot, and it is faced with the necessity of delegating a decision without full certainty one of these elements will be present.

First of all, if the committee does not have the facts or information on which to base its decision, management should either authorize the committee to commission the marshalling of the data or establish a task force with the expertise to supply the facts necessary to act. Second, selection of the participants is purely judgmental and arbitrary. Someone selected to serve as chair, for example, who is incapable, can be corrected through monitoring of the committee. The same applies to individual members, although normally it should be the responsibility of the committee chair to identify those committee members who are unable to participate, or obstruct the progress of the committee, so that they can be replaced. Lack of preparation for participatory management techniques has been discussed at some length previously, and management should have enough prescience not to include someone on the committee unfamiliar with these methods.

Sound working and organizational procedures pertain to supportive services the committee can expect, and a clear charge or set of goals. In the latter instance, management should never delegate a decision when the question being studied is unclear. The committee cannot be expected to deal with a problem that management cannot explain. Supportive services should also be reviewed with the committee chair or the full committee so the group does not waste time duplicating services that have already been provided for.

It is up to the committee itself to define alternatives. It often is essential that management specify in the charge to the committee that if alternatives cannot be identified as a basis for decision that this be reported before action is taken. That will warn management of potential problems or inadequate committee work.

Assuming that management does everything it can to ensure that the committee is prepared to arrive at a responsible decision, and yet the opposite occurs, then management is left with two clear alternatives. It can rescind the decision and undermine the participatory process, or allow it to be implemented. Which alternative should be taken has to be judged in terms of its impact upon the organization. If it is likely to be costly and create irreversible damage, then it is best to veto the committee decision, and take the heat. It is always possible to appoint another committee better prepared to make the decision, or simply to send the decision back to the original committee, asking them to respond to your objections before implementing the decision. If the irresponsible decision is relatively minor and will have little impact, then it might be best to let it proceed to its own fate. Generally, if it is that irresponsible, it will fall of its own accord.

Conflict Between Organizational and Individual Goals

Under participatory management, it would be a rare situation where individuals are given free rein to establish their own goals. Democracy is a shared process. When employees are hired and given assignments, they already accept some compromise. A person who is hired to serve as a cataloger does not have the freedom to become a reference librarian. Generally, the individual is given the opportunity to establish individual goals within the context of the job setting. When employees are given the opportunity to set personal goals, they should review them on a cooperative basis with their supervisor, who has the right to amend as necessary to ensure that the individual and the unit are going in the same direction.

Just as goal setting in a participatory environment is done jointly, individual goals must be negotiated between management and the employee. If that is understood at the start, there should be no friction. The usual cause of conflict is when either the supervisor or the individual is inflexible, at which point it is the responsibility of higher management to intercede. Under those circumstances the supervisor is advised of his or her misinterpretation, or the individual must be confronted with the decision that his or her goals are divergent from those of the library, and either some modification in personal goals is necessary or the individual should search for a more compatible institution.

There are also those instances where the employee makes a unilateral decision to adopt different goals. The same choices exist. There may be reason for flexibility or change in the unit's goals, or it may come to a decision on the part of the employee to adjust or leave the unit or organization.

The reference librarian who refuses to supply information on abortion to the public may have done so because she has modified her own goals in life and believes this information is immoral. However, she should not be allowed to alter the policies of the library to supply answers to all questions free of personal bias. There are usually goals arrived at jointly between management, employees, and governance, and the supervisor has an obligation to the organization to allow freedom of personal goals only within the parameters established by the organization. In a democratic form of management neither the individual nor the supervisor exercises unilateral or authoritarian decision making over the rights of others.

Responsibility for Implementation

Although we have treated decision making and implementation in this book interchangeably, there are many instances when the committee delegated authority for making the decision should not or cannot proceed to follow through with its implementation. Once a conclusion is reached, management's role is to see that the decision is carried out, and sometimes the committee is not the best vehicle to use.

It is a good principle in participatory management to delegate both decision making and follow-through to a committee at the unit level, where the employees and manager can best ensure the success of the change or immediately become aware of the deficiencies. System-wide policies may more properly be implemented through formal mechanisms established for that purpose. There will certainly be exceptions. Earlier in this book, a case study was presented involving implementation of a statewide multitype interlibrary plan for cooperation. The committee members actually assumed some roles in implementing that change because of the complexity of the task, their own enthusiasm, and their function as linking pins.

The steering committee or manager who appoints the members of a committee and prepares the charge of responsibilities to that committee will have to use judgment on how and who can best implement the decision based on their knowledge of the problem, the capabilities of the system, and the skills of the committee members. Responsibility for follow-through must then be stated in the charge. If the committee is granted authority to implement, then the manager can determine whether the committee has done its work through its reports or through the monitoring process established for the system, and take remedial action if the committee has failed in its responsibilities.

Confusion over who has responsibility to implement a delegated decision is one of the most common problems in participatory management, and although it is easy to correct as long as management understands its role, it can damage employee and management relations if it is forgotten. If a committee renders a decision with the understanding management will implement it, and nothing happens, the assumption is that participation was a sham and management has the policy on ice. On the other hand, management may reach the conclusion that staff are incapable of carrying through on a delegated responsibility and be reluctant to trust them in the future.

Time

Participatory management is not the most rapid means of making a decision. Management should be aware of that limitation and use the technique selectively for that reason. Time is required to ensure that the most appropriate participants are selected, prepared for their responsibility, and given time to go through their deliberations. It should be realized that while it is faster to reach a decision using more traditional techniques, in the long run time may be saved. A decision reached unilaterally can certainly cope with the problem immediately, but the long-term implications of that decision may lead to personnel problems, inefficiency, and poor service. The amount of time required can be reduced if 1/ the problem is clearly identified at the outset or the role and goals of the committee are understood thoroughly; 2/ a reasonable time frame is either stated as part of the charge or the committee is charged with responsibility to establish a time frame as rapidly as possible; and 3/ the participants are prepared to assume their assigned role and are familiar with participatory techniques. The experience and ability of the chair will also be critical, and selection of this individual by management or the group itself should be influenced by the time frame. Where time is not of the essence, but greater participation is essential, different leadership styles will be required. The reporting and monitoring process can also help in assessing whether correction is necessary to keep the group on schedule.

Resistance

The reluctance of either manager or the employee to work in a democratic fashion will demand the patience of the organization. Some middle managers interpret participation as a one-way street, where their chief executive is granting more flexibility to them to use whatever management styles they wish, including the authoritarian, and deny their employees similar flexibility in their work. There is a temptation for the chief executive to command major changes in supervisory style when this is discovered, which may only harden the attitude of the supervisor.

It is not unreasonable for a chief executive to ask supervisors what their attitude toward a proposed change is, when suspicion exists that democratic practice is not occuring. Sufficient experience with this may lead reluctant supervisors into confidence in their employees and in their own abilities to work in a democratic framework.

We have dealt elsewhere with the question of whether it is possible for any organization to function when only portions of the units employ participatory techniques, and it was noted that it is not only possible, but probable that many different management styles and systems will coexist in an institution. It is only when obvious harm is occuring that conformity may be required. Imposing one standard management technique upon an institution is the worst sort of tyranny and fails to recognize the different personalities of both managers and employees, as well as the differing nature of the tasks. Inevitably, the values as well as the pressures of participatory management will affect the reluctant supervisor or employee. Training and some experience with the technique on a trial basis may eliminate some of the mental barriers that exist.

It is possible that some individuals will never adapt to democratic methods, and in the final analysis management is left with the ultimate question of whether the organization can afford someone whose individual style clashes continuously with coworkers or supervisors. Through the evaluation process the individual can be counseled, and given indication that change is required for the health of the organization, or that his or her attitudes are affecting morale or hindering productivity. In some instances a transfer might provide the solution, but in too many instances managers resort to this approach to solve their individual unit's problem, but the organization is still left with it.

Traditionally, library directors confronted with employees or supervisors who created public relations problems in public service assignments banished those individuals into technical services. If individuals created problems in the previous setting because of an authoritarian attitude, they are certain to create problems in working conditions in the new setting.

Inappropriate Application

Not every problem or decision can be dealt with through participatory management. Time constraints may require an immediate decision, and some decisions which affect only an individual do not require group consideration. The average manager is faced with scores of decisions each day. It requires the judgment of that person, based on familiarity with the policies and goals of the organization, to determine when participation is desirable or required. It is a principle of democratic administration that the individual should be given responsibility for decisions involving his or her work assignments. It is also a principle that units should codetermine with management those policies which will affect the operation of each unit. Further, it should be a principle that the constituencies involved in an organization should participate on a representative basis in determining goals and policies affecting that organization. Another principle is that decisions involving two or more units should be reached jointly by representatives of those units.

That still leaves a broad gray area subject to the assessment of the manager. The decision reached by the middle manager and employees in a unit may well impact upon the organization, and it may require the intercession of the chief executive to ensure that collectively established goals are not adversely affected. In many instances the policy of the units and the organization blend so well that there is no need for delegation of a decision. Valid conclusions can be reached more efficiently by the manager through familiarity with those policies.

While productivity should be improved through the application of participatory techniques, an overapplication can have the opposite effect. Repeated meetings and continual delegation of policy questions can erode the time the worker and manager have to satisfy the requirements of their jobs and destroy the capability of the organization to carry out its goals. There is a continuum which exists in the democratization of any organization, ranging on one extreme to joint consideration of periodic questions to joint consideration of everything. Each organization has to arrive at its own state of equilibrium along that continuum, a condition where managers know that they have the consensus of their employees, and employees feel satisfied that they have effectively participated in decisions affecting their work and the policies of their organization. Anything more is excessive and inappropriate application of this technique.

Bureaucratic Tendencies

With its committee structures, group decision-making policies and techniques, various reports and communications practices, there is a tendency to establish a stifling bureaucracy which imposes yet another layer upon the organization, preventing it from flexibly responding to need and change. Generally, the freedom granted to the individual employee is offset by his or her assumption of increased responsibility to the unit and the organization.

In a profit-making organization there are countervailing pressures which prevent bureaucracy from taking hold. Overhead contributes to costs, which in turn affects the rate of return to the company and the economic return to the individual manager and employee. In the public sector these countervailing pressures are either not present or exert little influence upon the institution. For this reason it is desirable, if not essential, for an organization adopting democratic techniques to operate wherever possible as if it were a business, applying the principles of economic return to employees whenever possible.

The employees and supervisory staff of a library who realize that they can increase their own economic return in a democratic setting through streamlining procedures and elimination of bureaucratic paraphernalia are much more likely to achieve equilibrium. Indeed, the greatest danger in applying democratic management techniques in the public sector is that public sector managers might transfer only the form rather than the content of a method designed in the private sector to improve profit. In the public sector that can be perverted into a mechanism to increase bureaucracy.

Costs

This is clearly related to the aforementioned point, and the solution is the same. Whenever decision making is delegated, the cumulative impact of personnel time, communication, preparation, and implementation is certain to increase costs. While it can be argued that decisions are better when they are democratically reached, and in the long run will reduce costs, that does not solve short-run fiscal problems. The experience of some businesses and industries is that improved morale, less absenteeism, and increased productivity result from the application of this technique. Whether this is the result of a "Hawthorne effect," or other influences can not be determined, but there are mixed opinions in the academic and management sector about whether productivity really is increased. Certainly there would be more widespread adoption of the technique in the private sector if conclusive evidence existed.

Management should exercise some responsibility in the implementation of democratic techniques in making the participants aware of costs involved in the process. Committee meetings should be planned to maximize the use of individual time. Early in the conversion to participatory procedures, the steering committee should establish policies for the conduct of the participants aimed at controlling costs. Clear goals, written agendas, adherence to time schedules, determination of where consultation, reports, policies and similar documentation would be redundant will help control costs. Many organizations have created watchdog committees composed of both management and employees with the responsibility to oversee the activities of the organization in the area of costs, and this might be an effective device to harness the problem.

Beside the costs stimulated by the implementation and operation of democratic procedures, there is also the question of additional costs created by the decision-making groups. A unit may conclude that the only way in which it can increase productivity and improve working conditions will be through the purchase of new equipment. Multiply that decision by the number of units in the organization and the chief executive will suddenly discover that the democratic process can result in a dramatic increase in budget requests. Rather than falling back on authoritarian action, the best approach is to rely once again upon a democratic procedure which allows a priority list of needs to be established.

Personality Clashes

The portrait of a democratic manager reveals a self-reliant, inner-directed, high achiever who listens and accepts advice from employees. What should be done about these managers who do not fit that mold? As with the instance of the reluctant manager, there are grave problems in trying to impose a democratic management technique or style upon someone whose personality is entirely unreceptive.

The solution lies in an estimate of the ability of the individual to grow or change to meet new challenges. If an administrator believes that people are always fundamentally the same, and that while you may affect them you cannot permanently change them, then it would be best to counsel the individual and determine whether some accommodation can be reached. The turnover that often occurs when a new executive assumes responsibility for an organization is chiefly due to this conflict in management techniques and styles. Sometimes those who leave do so because of perceived or real beliefs that the incoming executive is less democratic than the predecessor.

Those administrators who believe, however, that individuals are capable of change and growth have a strong obligation to work toward familiarizing persons with new methods and granting them time to gain confidence and skill in its application. Anything other than this would contradict the principles of democratic management and deny opportunity to the individual manager to exercise freedom in work methods. The executive should establish the parameters within which a democratic technique will be employed, and provide preparation and training where necessary. Beyond that, the executive should grant flexibility to unit managers.

The executive who encounters a manager who appears to have a personality conflict in using democratic techniques should examine his or her own basis for reaching that determination. Is the manager unable to employ this style because of individual factors, or is the manager resisting merely because of a clash with the executive? Every manager or executive believes inherently that the method of management they employ is the most effective. Perhaps the best way to cope with managers who employ autocratic methods is to review with them the results they have achieved, compared with those who employ more democratic methods. This changes the setting from one in which the manager believes the executive is attempting to impose philosophies and methods to an effort to solve some problems in productivity and morale by drawing upon the successful experience of others.

Inevitably, there will always be those individuals who will not adjust well to a democratic mode of management. Some workers only respond to authoritarian leadership, and some supervisors lack confidence in their ability to lead when decisions are shared with their workers. The best advice is to work toward familiarizing them with the benefits and techniques, in the belief that they will grow. But at such time as counseling and training have failed, and attitudes or methods clash with the goals and policies of the institution, the executive has to remember the final obligation to the organization.

Uncertain Outcome

The reluctance many managers and employees have to accept participatory management is a perceived uncertainty in the outcome. In fact, one of the advantages of an authoritarian management is that it provides more security. The outcome of a decision may be equally uncertain, but if employees are not involved in that decision, they do not have to worry about the consequences. That is management's problem.

When employees and managers are involved in decision making the burden is shifted. If the decision was wrong, then the group will have to bear the burden. That can lead to reluctance to make the decision at all. Procrastination can occur in participatory settings just as in more traditional techniques. Some managers say that they have not delegated a decision because they are uncertain whether a committee could even reach a decision on the issue.

More often, managers are reluctant to delegate a decision because they are uncertain they can control the outcome. They believe that as long as they remain accountable for the actions of their unit, they better be certain of the outcome of a decision. The best way the organization can deal with this problem is to establish a policy that individuals will not be held accountable for decisions reached democratically. They will be held accountable only for their individual actions and responsibilities. In this fashion, the fear of both the supervisor and the committee regarding the possibility of an error will not prevent them from reaching a collective decision. It will motivate the supervisor to seek participation in decisions affecting the unit to ensure there is less likelihood of error. At the same time, it will not relieve individual members of the unit of the obligation to fulfill their responsibilities.

There is another dimension to this problem, and that is the uncertainty that the ultimate outcome of participatory management will enhance the future of the organization. That will be discussed in the next and final chapter. It should be sufficient here to say, however, that increasing democratic action in any institution places the ultimate responsibility in the hands of those who have the greatest stake in its future. That is a powerful incentive to assure the well being and continuing utility of the organization.

We have reviewed in this chapter various problems inherent in the democratic process. Irresponsible decisions and the conflict between the goals of the individual and the organization were dealt with in terms of their avoidance and solution. The question of assignment for implementation of decisions was considered in the context of both the committee and management. Time and cost control were viewed primarily from a management perspective through the suggestion of various methods designed to lessen their impact. Resistance to democratic techniques as well as personality clashes were considered primarily from a view that these are certain to arise, and methods for ameliorating their adverse influence on the organization were considered. It was noted that participatory methods are not a panacea and a number of simple principles were presented to aid the user in identifying the most appropriate situations for this management technique. Solutions to bureaucratic tendencies were proposed through greater application of economic return, and the problems of uncertainty in the outcome of delegated decision making were considered and solutions suggested through a reassessment of where responsibility for error should be placed.

As is evident, there are problems in this technique, as there are with any management method. Again, the principal advantage of democratic management is the flexibility and opportunity for solutions which it offers to the organization and its participants.

XI THE FUTURE OF PARTICIPATORY MANAGEMENT IN LIBRARIES

A POPULAR futurist, Alvin Toffler has a scenario in his book *The Third Wave* where all work is performed in the home.[1] Mother and father both have their on-line computer terminals connecting them to their respective workplaces, and the children are involved in the learning process through their terminals or interactive CATV systems with their educational institution. Toffler visualized a return to individual freedom in worklife, an electronic cottage industry, where most people would avoid the necessity to attend large factories or schools, and all would have flexibility in work methods and hours.

Some of this scenerio is actually occurring. In one midwestern library its public already functions on an interactive basis. There would be little problem installing similar terminals in the homes of the employees of that institution and allowing them to maintain access to the data bases and extend on-line services to the public from their own homes. Despite the probability of Toffler's scenario coming to pass, I believe that society will still require organizational techniques which ensure that people can work effectively together toward a common goal.

Participatory management does grant greater freedom for individuals to set their own methods, within the parameters established by the organization. That is certain to lead to greater motivation and increased satisfaction in one's career, as we have discussed in the theoretical justification for this tech-

169

nique elsewhere in this book. But the experience of society, both in the private and the public sector, is that as problems and goals, as well as technology employed to solve those problems and attain those goals, become more complex, we are increasingly required to draw upon more special skills, organizations, and constituencies. More group work will be required, not less.

There is a clear and pronounced trend toward participation in decision making, and as the need arises to develop long-range goals and plans it will become increasingly difficult for each of the constituencies, specialists, and managers, as well as those who will actually implement plans, to gain a voice in the planning process without increasing adoption of the participatory technique.

Clearly there will be more emphasis on representational methods, with design of techniques to ensure that workers will have the opportunity to elect spokespersons whenever they are unable to participate directly in decisions. In libraries we are likely to see more joint management-employee cabinets, and there are certain to be pressures to include worker representation in governance. Generally that has been avoided because of the public philosophy that user control over public institutions is essential to protect user interests. However, we have seen that the governance of most libraries is not representative of its actual users. As more decisions are made which require participation from employee groups, it is a natural trend that employees will take their place in the Board Room.

The imprint of participation on planning in libraries will probably be greater internal emphasis. The public library that continually added branches because of public pressure on its board provides a good example of the problem which was created by the lack of employee input in planning. Had that existed, evidence would have been presented that the institution was overextending itself and straining existing resources. While the director of the library presumably could and may have introduced that information, he or she is an employee charged with implementing the policy and plans of the Board. If the Board reached the policy decision to expand, then the director was charged to expand the system.

The danger of employee participation in policy setting and planning is the inherent conflict of interest which may arise. Clearly, the employee would favor salary increases over expansion of services, but that is where the balance of the Board would prevail. Trustees may become convinced that improved pay or working conditions are required, but this conclusion would be reached through joint deliberations. For this reason, as participation spreads throughout the library, there will be greater attention given to improvements in equipment, collections and services that already exist, since the staff will have a channel into the planning and decision-making process that did not exist before.

Whether that will be good or bad will be hard to predict. Many institutions could certainly benefit from a reallocation of priorities from further extension of service to users to correcting the deterioration which has occurred in facilities, collections, and working conditions. On the other hand, there may be tendency to terminate efforts, pathetic though they have been, to reach nonusers, such as the economically disadvantaged. If efforts continue to reform governance among institutions that provide greater opportunity for representation by users, that trend may be offset.

Planning in libraries is likely to be affected by participatory management techniques in two ways. There are certain to be more people at the planning table, and mechanisms to ensure representation from the various stakeholders will evolve to satisfy that need. Second, the path taken in planning will be increasingly influenced by the need to satisfy the internal needs of the institution.

Strategy in reaching specific decisions in libraries is certain to be critically altered. The classic example will be in collection building. Under more traditional techniques, the governing board established certain priorities or determined where strengths should be developed, and it then became the responsibility of management to respond through the development of formal policies and procedures. Professional staff who observed that demands were not being satisfied, and that collections were inappropriate to need, had little input or recourse. That situation has changed in many libraries, in that collection building is one aspect of library activity where participatory management is commonly practiced.

While democratic policies vest professionals with the opportunity to participate in collection building, and allow them the chance to purchase materials requested by users, there is still the need to reconcile their views with the opinions of governance. Collections may have been built in anticipation of curriculum changes or shifts in community economy as a result of information which was available to trustees and not known by professional staff. Management is then left with the role of developing methods for the opinions of all the constituencies to be brought together to allow collective decision making. Once again we see the value of involving the various parties in decisions. This is no different that the problem posed by input to planning, except for greater frequency of decisions.

It is easier to develop strategies for reaching consensus on matters which are likely to arise only periodically, such as a long-range plan, which might be revised annually. Working policies of the library, involving collection development and personnel administration, usually evolve continuously. The computer is likely to be a strong influence on the path that administrators take in arranging input and participation or policies requiring frequent interaction between varied constituencies. During the White House Conference on Libraries and Information Services, the participants made use of an interactive system which allowed entry of various resolutions and questions. Other participants having an interest in the subject, or anxious to provide input, could access this data and react to it. While this was a very informal and free-wheeling device for achieving communication on the issues, it is a harbinger of things to come when institutions such as libraries become more democratized.

The future shape of the library organization chart is also likely to be materially altered through greater democratization. A tenet of management has been the principle of the span of administrative control. Presumably each supervisor had only a limited number of assignments and staff to supervise because he or she could not adequately direct these efforts if the number exceeded some specific ratio. Often that was seven to one, but the literature varied as to the exact number since little empirical evidence existed as to what the administrative span should be, and the nature of the work often was a more important determinant. Administrative positions were then authorized like some recipe for baked goods, such as one division head for every seven units, etc.

As the library becomes more democratic, there will be greater responsibility placed on individual employees to arrange their work, inspect it, and see that assignments are completed in time to avoid delay for a coworker. Executives will be facing situations where attrition may allow them to eliminate supervisory positions as well as general positions as confidence in the ability of employees to shoulder these tasks increases, and as existing supervisors gain experience in the techniques necessary to operate with a larger number of employees. This tendency toward reduction in supervisory positions would be greatly expedited if more opportunity for economic return could be coupled with it. Employees and supervisors alike have little incentive to assume additional responsibilities unless governance and executive-level personnel cooperate in providing such incentives.

The library as an institution has always had concern for greater flexibility in response to community needs, and the future shift to more use of participatory techniques should only further contribute to greater responsiveness to the user. Under more traditional management techniques there were often so many layers and cushions between the user and the policy-making level of the agency that changes often occurred long after the need arose. Because the library is an institution with close links between the professional staff and the user, any opportunity in organizational redesign which places the professional in a decision-making position regarding policy should allow for superior service, more rapid response, and less waste.

Despite the argument that larger library systems operate more efficiently because of the economy of scale, most library administrators will admit that smaller institutions are superior, chiefly because of the proximity of the professional serving the user to the policy-making level. The director of a small public library, who also serves on the reference desk several days a week, is going to communicate to the board much more accurately what the public is demanding in terms of services, collections, and facilities, than the director of an institution which has five levels of supervisors. It is true that many administrators devote some time on occasion to working directly with the public in an effort to counteract that isolation, but this can never substitute for the daily experience that a public service librarian receives. As a partner in decisions on policies involving service to the user, that public services librarian is going to be far more effective than an administrator who dabbles at the service desk several times a year.

Libraries should also become better able to integrate the work of one unit with another in the future through the application of democratic techniques. As an example, there is the long-standing practice of many libraries to schedule catalogers in reference and similar public service positions. The practice was designed to keep those individuals sensitive to the demands of the user and the relative capability of the catalog to supply necessary bibliographic information. While that was not a bad expedient, and it certainly provided some variety and possibly job enrichment, it is not as effective as setting policy for certain cataloging practices cooperatively. It seems logical that a cataloger knows the science of cataloging best, and the reference librarian should know the best method of satisfying the user's needs. Therefore, if they are provided with greater opportunity to work together in solving problems and making decisions, this should result in a vastly improved catalog for the benefit of the user.

Although there are some countervailing elements, the introduction of participatory management in libraries should provide for more creative services, given adequate opportunity for financing of these innovations. If libraries are successful in winning a better share of the tax dollar, there is a synergistic effect whenever a variety of people work toward solving common problems. I will always recall the experience of one library director who could not solve a vexing problem of vandalism. Almost everyday graffiti would be carved, spray painted, or etched into the front of the building, and every effort he made seemed to have little impact. One day he called in the custodian and the children's librarian, and asked for their suggestions. The children's librarian indicated that she knew who the vandals were, and explained that their parents worked the late evening shift at a local factory so they were left to their own devices. The custodian indicated that the last bus did not come until 10 or 15 minutes after the library closed and the children had to be evicted. After some discussion, the group decided that maybe the solution would be to occupy the children in some fashion until the bus arrived and it was decided that they could organize a young volunteers group. The children were approached with the idea, and they promptly enrolled. The idea later spread and the group grew both in size and popularity to provide lasting benefit to the library. Incidentally, the graffiti stopped.

Bringing more of the constituents to focus on a decision will not only provide more creative ideas, but should also ensure that they will work, since the participants will have greater commitment to the ideas. Discussions with winners of the John Cotton Dana Library Publicity Awards over a several year period regarding the origin of their award-winning creative ideas revealed that each of the institutions practiced a high level of democractic management, and the public relations programs were generally arrived at through the synergistic impact of many individuals from different levels and units of the institution.

The future use of democratic management techniques should contribute to the solution of one of the most vexing management problems, that of work standards and employee evaluation. Every supervisor has a different standard for individual work, and there are enormous inconsistencies which appear in employee evaluations. While there is usually a review opportunity by a superior, invariably supervisors will argue that they are in a better position to judge the quantity and quality of work of an employee under their immediate direction.

The democratic organization should allow employees and managers to develop work standards which are consistent, and which can then be applied fairly in the evaluation process. At the same time, the future should hold greater likelihood of management evaluation by employees. As employees and supervisors gain confidence in working together resolving problems as equals, there will be greater willingness to use the evaluation process to identify individual problems in working relationships. Supervisors have been saying for years that the evaluation process is good for the employee since it defines where improvement is needed. That same sauce should be good for the supervisor. In libraries this process is not likely to extend to employee removal of supervisors or to their election by employees.

There is an important relationship which must be maintained between employer and employee, and that holds true throughout the various levels in an organization. The supervisor is paid to coordinate the work of a unit or units in an organization, and there are times when responsibilities to the organization must override the needs of the unit. The middle manager may not be able to pursue the group will of the unit because their decision conflicts with the goals and policies of the organization. That may make supervisors unpopular, and yet they will be effective in their assignments. For this reason there is an inherent conflict of interest which occurs when the unit elects or hires its own supervisor. The supervisor maintains the equilibrium of the unit in the organization, and when the employee assumes responsibility for supervisory appointment, the equilibrium is lost.

Clearly, economic trends will have a profound impact upon libraries in the future and more democratic management may face some tests. History will demonstrate that organizations in crisis usually centralize decision making and policy determination. That is especially true in the public sector. Municipalities, school districts, and academic institutions which have undergone fiscal crises in recent years usually lost control over their budgets and long-range planning powers to fiscal oversight panels with powers to veto the decisions of normal governance. A parallel change then took place within the institution, as unit after unit was divested of decision-making powers.

The impact upon democratic management practices in those situations is difficult to assess at this writing because of the limited number of examples. In several of those institutions the level of democratic decision making was not at a notably visible level when the crisis occurred. It can be assumed that if a library operating at a high level of democratic management fell into a fiscal crisis, governance would be less likely to trust the decisions which it had delegated to lower levels in the organization, and may rescind that delegation. However, it could also be that these lower-level units practicing more democracy were more efficient, but could not participate in the policy decisions at the higher level in the library to permit corrective action to occur and prevent the crisis. Only future research can determine whether democratic management techniques are hindered in the public sector as more and more units of government experience economic crises, or whether greater democratization is encouraged in an effort to control costs and increase productivity.

Democratic management will also confront the certain tendency of greater regulation through imposition of new federal and state controls. Neither the public nor the private sector will be immune, despite federal policy changes. In discussion with the staff of a public-library branch undergoing renovation there was a good example of the conflict. The branch was given authority to develop its own building program, but the architect had to make numerous revisions to satisfy recent federal guidelines guaranteeing that the handicapped would have access to all levels of the building. The staff objected and through its administrative staff attempted to exercise its decision-making powers over the design of the building. They failed; the federal regulations prevailed.

Perhaps greater citizen participation in federal and state governments may lead to more flexible regulations, or the granting of greater opportunity for compromises to be reached at the local level. In this example, the branch happens to have a strong program of service to handicapped people; if they could have worked on a solution which would permit satisfactory access to the handicapped people in that community, it would have been a better solution to the problem.

The education of librarians should be considerably influenced by democratic trends in the future. While many graduate institutions have introduced democracy into the curriculum, and others have also introduced it into the classroom and operational methods of the school, others are hindered by restrictions imposed by academic bureaucracies. As these bureaucracies are affected by trends for greater participatory opportunity in society at large, students should gain more experience with the technique and be prepared to effectively use opportunities for decision making upon placement. Professional students commonly evaluate their instructors in library school, but find that they do not do so for supervisors when they get on the job.

Traditionally, graduate institutions have been somewhat ahead of libraries in the teaching of new management techniques which may have only been partially introduced or not used at all by library administrators. Several methods are employed to keep the graduate school and the field in closer coordination. For example, the opportunities for administrators to teach in graduate schools, and opportunities granted to faculty to work in the field, enhance mutual understanding. Nonetheless, students continually express disappointment when they find that the libraries in which they are placed practice administrative techniques less democractic than those discussed in their professional training. Similarly, library administrators complain about the lack of preparation many new graduates receive in school regarding the responsibilities they will have to assume, and their inability to effectively administer units using the technique employed at the library.

While there will always be some conflict between the curriculum and practice, participatory management provides a method of narrowing that gap and helping both the graduate school and the library to serve the public more effectively and permit greater job satisfaction to the librarian. Both the graduate school and the library need to meet more regularly to review common problems. The annual conferences rarely do more than allow the individuals involved in the same activities to share experiences. Library administrators talk with library administrators and library educators talk with library educators. The bridge is the student, and perhaps some future date will witness tripartite conferences between library school faculty, students, and administrators discussing what steps can be taken to help improve library training, administration, and library service through more democratic procedures.

In this book I have sought to provide some practical insight into the use of more democratic techniques in library administration. I have drawn from business and industry as well as the library profession, and upon my own experiences and observations. No single management system is satisfactory for all situations, and individual personality traits and strengths will more typically determine whether an individual manager will select an authoritarian or a democratic process in completing an assignment. But every supervisor must be influenced by the work setting and the background attitudes of the individuals involved in that task.

We are fortunate to live in a democracy, and that should provide ample evidence of what a more democratic approach can accomplish if the same philosophy is applied in the workplace. America has lived through many crises. While there have been some strains and modifications in the system, we have fundamentally remained a democracy for more than two hundred years, granting to the citizens of this nation the opportunity to pursue individual goals, granting them challenges for growth, providing them with incentives to live rich and meaningful lives. That philosophy has produced, to this day, one of the most productive and efficient nations in history. I hope there may be some who read this book who will believe that the translation of these techniques to the library may result in similar benefits.

Reference

1. Toffler, Alvin. *The Third Wave*. New York, Morrow, 1980.

BIBLIOGRAPHY

Allen, George R. "Liberty, Equality and Anxiety at Worker-Run International Group Plans," *Business and Society Review*, Winter 1977-8, p. 43-46.

Appelbaum, Steven H. "Human Resource Development: A Foundation for Participative Leadership," *Personnel Administrator*, March 1979, p. 50-56.

Arbose, Jules. "Where Workers Choose Their Own Managers," *International Management*, February 1978, p. 34-35, 38, 40.

Argyris, Chris. *Integrating the Individual and the Organization*, New York, John Wiley, 1964.

―――. *Personality and Organization*, New York, Harper and Row, 1957.

Austin, David L. "Portrait of a Personnel Executive: More Participation," *Personnel Administrator*, August 1978, p. 58-63.

Bass, Bernard M., and Shackleton, V. J. "Industrial Democracy and Participative Management: A Case for a Synthesis," *Academy of Management Review*, July 1979, p. 393-404.

Bass, Lawrence W. *Management by Task Forces: A Manual on the Operation of Interdisciplinary Teams*, Mt. Airy, Md., Lomond Books, 1975.

Bernstein, Paul. *Workplace Democratization: Its Internal Dynamics*, Kent, Ohio, Kent State University, Comparative Administration Research Institute, 1976.

181

Blumberg, Paul. *Industrial Democracy: The Sociology of Participation*, London, Constable, 1968.

Booz, Allen, and Hamilton, Inc. *Organization and Staffing of Libraries of Columbia University: A Case Study*, Westport, Conn. Redgrave Information Resources Corp., 1973.

Brewer, Richard. "Personnel's Role in Participation," *Personnel Management*, September 1978, p. 27–29, 45.

―――. "Realities of Participation," *Management Today*, October 1978, p. 90–93.

Business Week. "GM's Test of Participation," February 23, 1976, p. 88–90.

―――. "How to Promote Productivity," July 24, 1978, p. 146, 151.

Cliche, Paul. "The Montreal Citizen's Movement Project: Transforming the City Library into a Network of Community Centres Run by Local Citizens," *Argus*, May–August 1978, p. 59–62.

Craig, Mark S. "Worker Alienation—Is Management Participation a Solution?" *Industrial Management*, January–February 1979, p. 22–25.

Curley, Douglas G. "Employee Sounding Boards: Answering the Participative Need," *Personnel Administrator*, May 1978, p. 69–73.

Dachler, H. Peter. "Conceptual Dimensions and Boundaries of Participation in Organizations: A Critical Evaluation," *Administrative Science Quarterly*, March 1978, p. 1–39.

Davidson, David S. "Employee Participation Can Mean Increased Employee Satisfaction," *Supervisory Management*, February 1979, p. 33–36.

Dickinson, Dennis W. "Some Reflections on Participative Management in Libraries," *College and Research Libraries*, July 1978, p. 253–262.

Dickson, John W. "The Participation Gaps," *Management Today*, July 1978, p. 46–49.

Dickson, Paul. *The Future of the Workplace: The Coming Revolution in Jobs*. New York, Weybright and Talley, 1975.

Driscoll, James W. "Trust and Participation in Organizational Decision Making as Predictors of Satisfaction," *Academy of Management Journal*, March 1978, p. 44–56.

Drucker, Peter F. *The Practice of Management*, New York, Harper and Row, 1954.

_____. *The Effective Executive*, New York, Harper and Row, 1966.

Dudek, Daniel H. "Multiple Management," *Advanced Management Journal*, Spring 1979, p. 26–31.

Fischer, Russel G. "Workers' Self-Management and Libraries," *Canadian Library Journal*, June 1977, p. 165, 167, 169–171.

Fisher, David T. "Worker Participation in West German Industry," *Monthly Labor Review*, May 1978, p. 59–63.

Flener, Jane G. "Newer Approaches to Personnel Management," Paper presented at the General Council Meeting of the International Federation of Library Associations, Washington, D. C., November 16–23, 1974.

Ford, Robert N. *Motivation Through the Work Itself*, New York, American Management Association, 1969.

Fox, William M. "Limits to the Use of Consultative-Participative Management," *California Management Review*, Winter 1977, p. 17–22.

Fredriksson, Inger. "Are You Allowed to Join in the Decision Making?" *Biblioteksbladet*, August 1977, p. 133–136.

Frost, Carl F. "The Scanlon Plan: Anyone for Free Enterprise?" *MSU Business Topics*, Winter 1978, p. 25–33.

Garson, G. David, and Smith, Michael P. eds. *Organizational Democracy: Participation and Self-Management*, Beverly Hills, Calif., Sage Publications, 1975.

Ghosh, Pradip K., and Van de Vall, Mark. "Workers' Participation in Management—Applied," *Management International Review*, Fall 1978, p. 55–68.

Hall, Jay, and Glasgow, Robert K. "Portrait of the Manager as an Achiever," *Supervisory Management*, August 1979, p. 10–14.

Halse, J. "Does Workers' Participation in Management Lead to Better Service to Readers?" *Bibliotek*, October 1975, p. 241–242.

Heller, Frank. "Realities of Participation," *Management Today*, March 1978, p. 74–77, 153.

Herbst, Ph. G. *Alternatives to Hierarchies*, Leiden, Martinus Nijhoff, 1976.

Heron, Alexander. *Why Men Work*, Palo Alto, Stanford University Press, 1948.

Herzberg, Frederick. *Work and the Nature of Man*, London, Staples Press, 1968.

————; Bernard Mauser; and Barbara Bloch Snyderman. *The Motivation to Work*, New York, John Wiley and Sons, 1959.

————. "Participation is Not a Motivator," *Industry Week*, September 4, 1978, p. 38–40, 44.

Jenkins, David. *Job Power: Blue and White Collar Democracy*, Garden City, N.Y., Doubleday, 1973.

Kaplan, Louis. "The Literature of Participation: From Optimism to Realism," *College and Research Libraries*, November 1975, p. 473–479.

————. "On Decision Sharing in Libraries: How Much Do We Know?" *College and Research Libraries*, January 1977, p. 25–31.

Keppler, Robert H. "What the Supervisor Should Know About Participative Management," *Supervisory Management*, May 1978, p. 34–40.

Koch, James L. "The Industrial Relations Setting, Organizational Forces and the Form and Content of Worker Participation," *Academy of Management Review*, July 1978, p. 572–583.

LaBerge, Roy. "Adelaide International Conference," *Labour Gazette*, November–December 1978, p. 510–511.

———. "Some Lessons From Sweden," *Labour Gazette*, September 1978, p. 398–399.

Lawler, Edward E., III, *Pay and Organizational Effectiveness*, New York, McGraw-Hill, 1971.

Lederer, Victor. "Decision Making: Should Employees Get In On the Act?" *Administrative Management*, September 1978, p. 51–52, 58–62.

Lesieur, Frederick G. *The Scanlon Plan*, Cambridge, Mass., M.I.T. Press, 1958.

Lewis, George R. *Professional Staff Participation in the Decision-Making Process in Selected University Libraries*, Washington, D.C., EDRS, 1975.

Likert, Rensis. *New Patterns of Management*, New York, McGraw-Hill, 1961.

———. *The Human Organization*, New York, McGraw-Hill, 1967.

Lincoln, James F. *Incentive Management*, Cleveland, The Lincoln Electric Co., 1951.

Long, Richard J. "Desires For and Patterns of Worker Participation in Decision Making After Conversion to Employee Ownership," *Academy of Management Journal*, September 1979, p. 611–617.

Lowry, Charles B. *The ACRL Standards and Library Governance, a Comparison of the Personnel Systems of Five Major Academic Libraries,* Master's Thesis, Chapel Hill, NC, University of North Carolina, Graduate School of Library Science, 1974.

———. *Report of the Proposed Library Reorganization.* Charlotte, N.C., North Carolina University, J. Murrey Atkins Library, 1975.

Lundine, Stanley N. "Labor, Management and the Proposed Human Resources Development Act," *Employee Relations Law Journal,* Spring 1978, p. 467–474.

McCormick, Charles P. *The Power of People,* New York, Harper and Brothers, 1949.

McGrath, William E. *Development of a Long Range Strategic Plan for a University Library; The Cornell Experience: Chronicle and Evaluation of the First Year's Effort,* Ithaca, N.Y., Cornell University Libraries, 1973.

McGregor, Douglas. *The Human Side of Enterprise,* New York, McGraw-Hill, 1960.

Marchant, Maurice P. *Participative Management in Academic Libraries,* Westport, Conn., Greenwood Press, 1976.

Marrow, Alfred J., Bowers, David G. and Seashore, Stanley E. *Management by Participation,* New York, Harper and Row, 1967.

Marrow, Alfred. "Participatory Management—The Next Step for Corporations," *Manage,* November/December, 1976, p. 24–25, 30.

Martin, Allie Beth, Swartz, Rod and Marchant, Maurice. *Participatory Management* (Audio Cassette) (Tulsa, OK, Tulsa City-County Public Library, 1972?)

Maslow, Abraham. *Motivation and Personality,* New York, Harper and Row, 1970.

Mayo, Elton. *The Human Problems of an Industrial Civilization*, Boston, Harvard University, Graduate School of Business Administration, 1946.

Megalli, Bill and Sanderson, G. "Productivity-Quality of Working Life a Key Factor?" *Labour Gazette*, November–December 1978, p. 500–504.

Millar, Jean A. "Organization Structure and Worker Participation," *Personnel Review*, Spring 1979, p. 14–19.

Murray, Thomas J. "More Power for the Middle Manager," *Dun's Review*, June 1978, p. 60–62.

Musmann, Victoria Kline, "Managerial Style in the Small Public Library," *California Librarian*, July 1978, p. 7–20.

Myers, M. Scott. *Every Employee a Manager*, New York, McGraw-Hill, 1970.

Naor, Jacob. "Planning By Consensus—A Participative Approach to Planning," *Advanced Management Journal*, Autumn 1978, p. 40–47.

Northrup, Bowen. "More Swedish Firms Attempt to 'Enrich' Production Line Jobs," *Wall Street Journal*, October 25, 1974, p. 1.

Nyren, Karl. "Skirmish Line: Participatory Management in Libraries: What Is Its Future?" *Library Journal*, May 15, 1976, p. 1186–1187.

Papin, Jean-Pascal and Fitch, Gordon. "Participative Management by Objectives," *Management International Review*, 1977, p. 69–75.

Parkym, Brian. "Democracy, Accountability and Participation," *Industrial and Commercial Training*, August 1978, p. 318–321.

Perkins, Ralph A. "The Creative Act and Leadership in Manpower Programs: A Synergistic Approach," *Adherent*, December 1978, p. 33–39.

Porket, J. L. "Industrial Relations and Participation in Management in the Soviet-Type Communist System," *British Journal of Industrial Relations*, March 1978, p. 70–85.

Portis, Bernard. "Managers Consider Employee Participation as a Means of Improving Productivity," *Business Quarterly*, Winter 1977, p. 5, 8–9, 11.

Quick, Thomas L. "Likert's System for Participative Management," *Training*, July 1978, p. 52.

Robbins, Jane. *Citizen Participation and Public Library Policy*, Metuchen, N.J., Scarecrow Press, 1975.

Sandhu, Sarbjit. "Group Participation in the Academic Libraries," *Indian Librarian*, June 1976, p. 40–44.

Schaeffer, Dorothy. "Management by Objectives," *Supervision*, July 1978, p. 4–5.

Shaffer, Kenneth. "The Library Administrator as Negotiator: Exit the 'Boss,'" *Library Journal*, September 1, 1975, p. 1475–80.

Shaughnessy, Thomas W. "Participative Management, Collective Bargaining and Professionalism," *College and Research Libraries*, March 1977, p. 140–146.

Smith, Eldred. "Do Libraries Need Managers?," *Library Journal*, February 1, 1969, p. 502–506.

Swaak, Reyer A. "Industrial Democracy: An Update," *Personnel Administrator*, April 1978, p. 34, 40–41, 45.

Taylor, Frederick Winslow. *Scientific Management*, New York, Harper and Row, 1947.

Toffler, Alvin. *The Third Wave*, New York, Morrow, 1980.

Townsend, Robert. *Up the Organization*, Greenwich, Conn., Fawcett, 1970.

Vroom, Victor H. *Work and Motivation*, New York, John Wiley, 1964.

Wainwright, David. "Launching into Participation," *Personnel Management*, December 1978, p. 28–33, 43.

Walfish, Beatrice. "Participative Management Boosts Productivity," *Manage*, March/April 1978, p. 17–19.

Walker, Kenneth F. "Workers' Participation in Management," Paper presented at Second World Congress of International Industrial Relations Association, Geneva, September 1–4, 1970.

Walton, Richard E., and Leonard A. Schlesinger. "Do Supervisors Thrive in Participative Work Systems," *Organizational Dynamics*, Winter 1979, p. 25–38.

White, J. Kenneth. "The Scanlon Plan: Causes and Correlates of Success," *Academy of Management Journal*, June 1979, p. 292–312.

Whyte, William H., Jr. *The Organization Man*, New York, Simon and Schuster, 1956.

Williams, Ervin, ed. *Participative Management: Concepts, Theory and Implementation*, Atlanta, Georgia State University, School of Business Administration, 1976.

Wolff, Michael F. "Whatever Happened to 'Participative' Management?" *IEEE Spectrum*, February 1979, p. 60–68.

Wood, Muriel B. "The Organization of Successful Participative Management in a Health Sciences Library," *Bulletin. Medical Library Association*, April 1977, p. 216–223.

Yavarkovsky, Jerome and Haas, Warren J. *The Columbia University Management Program*, Paper presented at the General Council Meeting of the International Federation of Library Association, Washington, D.C., November 1974.

Zemke, Ron. "What Are High Achieving Managers Really Like?," *Training*, February 1979, p. 35–36.

INDEX